# PRACTICAL
# CAMPING
## HANDBOOK

# PRACTICAL CAMPING
## HANDBOOK

How to get the most from camping – everything from planning your trip to setting up camp and cooking outdoors, with over 350 step-by-step photographs

## PETER G. DRAKE

southwater

**Dedication:** To my parents, who gave me my first chance to travel to wild places; to Kate who has helped me so much to continue travelling over the last 30 years, and to Neil and Colin who have made some of the expeditions special because they were there with me.

This edition is published by Southwater
an imprint of Anness Publishing Ltd
Hermes House, 88–89 Blackfriars Road
London SE1 8HA
tel. 020 7401 2077; fax 020 7633 9499

www.southwaterbooks.com; www.annesspublishing.com

If you like the images in this book and would like to investigate using them for publishing, promotions or advertising, please visit our website www.practicalpictures.com for more information.

UK agent: The Manning Partnership Ltd sales@manning-partnership.co.uk

UK distributor: Grantham Book Services Ltd
orders@gbs.tbs-ltd.co.uk

North American agent/distributor: National Book Network
www.nbnbooks.com

Australian agent/distributor: Pan Macmillan Australia
customer.service@macmillan.com.au

New Zealand agent/distributor: David Bateman Ltd tel. (09) 415 7664; fax (09) 415 8892

Publisher: Joanna Lorenz
Editorial Director: Helen Sudell
Senior Editor: Sarah Ainley
Photographer: Martyn Milner
Designer: Nigel Partridge
Illustrator: Peter Bull Art Studio
Editorial Reader: Jay Thundercliffe
Production Controller: Steve Lang

### ETHICAL TRADING POLICY

Because of our ongoing ecological investment programme, you, as our customer, can have the pleasure and reassurance of knowing that a tree is being cultivated on your behalf to naturally replace the materials used to make the book you are holding. For further information about this scheme, go to www.annesspublishing.com/trees

Previously published as part of a larger volume,
*The Complete Practical Guide to Camping, Hiking and Wilderness Skills*

### PUBLISHER'S NOTE

### ACKNOWLEDGEMENTS

The publishers would like to thank the following individuals for their valuable contributions to this book:

Text advisors: Nick Banks, Peter Tipling, Dr Bill Turner, J. Evans, Mrs A. Funnel.

Advice and assistance: Malcolm Creasey, Sue Dowson, Andy Middleton, David Williams.

Models for photography: Doncaster Scout Group, Joe O'Brian, Robert Driskel, Mr and Mrs Gibson, Lynn Milner.

With special thanks to Julian McIntosh at Safariquip, The Stones, Castleton, Derbyshire (tel: 01433 620 320) for the loan of camping and walking equipment for photography, and to Andrew Morrison for the loan of additional camping items.

### PICTURE CREDITS

All the photography in this book is by Martyn Milner except for the following:

t = top; c = centre; b = bottom; l = left; r = right

Peter G. Drake: p16 (both), p17tl, p17tm, p17tr, p18 (both), p19t, p19br, p23 (both), p24bl, p49tl, p53bm, p53br, p60 (both), p61 (both), p62, p63 (both), p65, p66, p67tl, p67bl, p67br, p68bl, p69tl, p94bl, p95tr, p95br, p82t, p87t, p92br, p93 (both).

# CONTENTS

# INTRODUCTION

Camping has never been more popular than it is today. The lure of the Great Outdoors seems to have captivated people all over the world. If you've been bitten by the camping bug, whether you want to explore the wilderness and sleep under the stars, or just get a bit closer to nature by spending a few nights under canvas, this book will show you everything you need to know to get started.

Ironically, the pure fact of visiting the countryside, particulary fragile environments, can lead to their destruction. People wishing to go to wild unspoilt areas, to get back to a simpler, more natural life, can unfortunately have a detrimental impact on them, especially if visiting in a large group. It is a balancing act that must be achieved in order to protect the natural environment. Following a few basic principles, set out below, will help you to enjoy the countryside without destroying it or spoiling it for future visitors.

▼ *Travelling to a remote area alone and without backup makes you more vulnerable; plan your trip carefully to minimize risks.*

**Protecting the environment:**
• always dispose of rubbish in receptacles provided or take it away with you;
• use a stove for cooking, only build a fire if necessary and unrestricted, keep it small and use the minimum of dead wood locally available;
• keep to paths where possible and don't cross hedges or walls unless there are stiles or gates.

**When camping in the wild:**
• get permission from the landowner, unless you intend to camp on 'common land';
• use a trowel to bury human waste at least 30 metres/100 feet away from running water or lakes;
• move your tent after two nights to avoid damaging vegetation underneath;
• keep to small groups of one or two tents to minimize disturbance.

All successful camping trips start with proper planning. The less you know about the area you wish to camp in, the more research you need to do in order to be adequately prepared.

The first thing to consider is how you are going to get to the area you intend to camp at. If you are travelling

▲ *Carrying all your camping equipment on your back allows you to travel far away from civilization and stop where you like.*

by car or minibus, you will be less restricted in what you can take with you than if you are travelling by public transport or by plane.

Secondly, you need to think about what you intend to do while on the trip. Will you be hiking between campsites each day and need to carry all your equipment with you? Maybe you intend to cycle or canoe, in which case you need appropriate clothing and equipment for these activities.

Remember to plan the budget – even the simplest camping trip has costs attached. The main expenses to consider are equipment (purchase or hire), transport to the campsite (and/or from site to site), insurance, food, campsite charges and other living costs.

Depending on where you are going to camp there may be medical implications, such as vaccinations, additional equipment, or specialist clothing. You will also need an adequate stock of first aid supplies if camping in a remote area.

It is wise to think about what you will eat on your camping trip beforehand. If you are going to camp

in a wild area, you will more than likely need to take food with you. If you are going for a week or more, this may amount to a large quantity, in which case you will need to think about transporting the food. If your

▼ *A makeshift barbecue can easily be made with a metal grill and some rocks to support it and enclose the fire.*

▲ *The simple pleasures of sleeping under canvas and enjoying the freedom of the countryside cannot be over-estimated.*

trip is going to be based somewhere where food is readily available, you can buy supplies when you arrive or on a daily basis. However you may still want to bring any items that you can't live without! Remember that the amount of food you need to eat each day may be more than usual, especially if your trip involves physical activity, such as hiking or cycling, during the day.

When planning what to eat, consider how long it will take to cook. If you have a busy schedule each day, you may not want to spend a long time cooking meals. Finally, ensure that you include foods from all the main food groups to meet your nutritional requirements.

A basic necessity, but one which can easily be overlooked, is the availability of water. If you are staying at a campsite, there will doubtless be drinking water available on tap and most probably hot water for bathing as well. However, if you are intending to camp in the wild you will not have this

luxury. You need to plan where you will be able to get supplies of water and whether or not it will need purifying. Ensure that you take the necessary equipment for sterilizing water and suitable containers for carrying or storing it in.

Many of these issues are covered in more detail in the pages that follow. The book is split into two sections: Basic Equipment and Orienteering & Campcraft. The first part describes the most suitable equipment to take with you for a thoroughly enjoyable trip. The second part explains how to stay there comfortably and safely, as well as giving you the skills to use a map and navigate between locations. Even the best planned trips can go wrong so always have a back-up plan.

Remember that while we all want to have fun outdoors, we must respect our environment and preserve its unique quality for others. It is useful to bear the following adage in mind: 'take only memories, leave only footprints'. That way future generations will be able to experience and enjoy the unique environments that we can today.

# BASIC EQUIPMENT

Camping and orienteering equipment is now so developed that it is possible to travel and camp in considerable comfort. However, some items are expensive and may be too specialist for your needs. The key to being well equipped is to take what is necessary. Do not take more than you have to: this is especially important if you are backpacking. In the following pages the most essential equipment is discussed.

# Choosing your Equipment

Having the correct basic equipment is important for your comfort and safety. When assessing what you need, you should consider the climate and terrain of the area you are visiting and the activities planned. You also need to know how you are going to carry your gear, as this will affect the amount of weight and bulk you can manage.

### HOW TO ACQUIRE EQUIPMENT

Outdoor equipment suppliers sell for every possible climate and terrain, so if you are buying new items for your trip, consider what design features will serve you best to help narrow the choice. Many items are expensive, and most people build up their equipment over a number of years to spread the cost. If this is your first trip, try to borrow as much as you can from friends or a local walking or activity group. That way you will also gain from the experience of others, who will be able to tell you what is and what is not important. Have an understanding in writing with the owner on what items cost and how you will compensate them for lost, stolen or damaged items, and make sure you are sufficiently insured.

▼ *Wearing a helmet, gloves and suitable clothing and footwear is important for any cycling trip, even if the distance is short.*

### CLOTHING AND FOOTWEAR

The purpose of outdoor clothing is to keep you comfortable in the weather conditions you experience on your trip. It cannot be stressed enough that clothes need to be appropriate for the climate you will be operating in. Besides this, clothes need to be durable and quick drying, lightweight and low in bulk – this is especially important if you are carrying your gear in a pack on your back. Footwear has to protect your feet from water, mud, sand and rocks, while still enabling you to carry out your activities safely. Never be tempted to compromise your safety and comfort for fashion: it will make your trip a miserable one and may even put your life in danger.

### PERSONAL CAMP KIT

Your camp kit is the core items of equipment that you take with you on any trip to the wilderness, such as a compass, map, water bottle, wristwatch, cooking equipment and wash kit. Some items, such as a compass, are essential and you shouldn't set off without them. Other items, such as an inflatable pillow, are luxuries that you can do without if your weight/space allowance is limited. Group kit may include study materials, or catering-size cooking equipment. For more information, *see the section on* Personal Camp Kit.

### BASIC SURVIVAL KIT

In an emergency situation, having a few key items with you can make the difference between life and death. For information about what to include, *see the section on* Basic Survival Kit.

### TENTS

Probably the most expensive item on your list will be a tent, so be clear about what sort you need. The perfect tent is weatherproof, spacious, easy to pitch, light and compact to carry, but few tents are all of these things and you will need to decide how to compromise. For more information, *see the section on* Choosing a Tent.

▲ *For backpacking trips you need cooking and sleeping equipment that is light in weight and designed to be packed up small.*

### SLEEPING EQUIPMENT

The right sleeping gear can mean the difference between a good night's rest and a bad one. Consider where and in what conditions you will be using your sleeping bag, then buy the best one you can afford. For more information, *see the section on* Sleeping Bags.

### BACKPACKS

A backpack has to allow you to carry your equipment in comfort, and what sort of backpack you need will depend on your activities and how much you need to carry. Features such as hip belts, padding, frames or side straps can be very useful but they can also add weight and cost. For more information, *see the section on* Backpacks.

### TOOLS

When living outdoors it is very useful to have some tools with you, even if your tool kit consists of nothing more than a penknife. Check with the police to see if any of your tools are illegal. If you have a machete, large knife or flares, for example, you may be able to own them but not carry them around in public. Anything that is classed as a firearm will need an official firearms certificate. For more information, *see the section on* Tools.

## BASIC HIKING AND CAMPING EQUIPMENT CHECKLIST

The following kit list is for a walking and camping trip lasting 3–4 weeks in a temperate climate:

### Clothing and footwear
Underwear
Thermal vest, long johns and
    long-sleeved undershirt
Cotton T-shirts
Cotton socks
Woollen socks
Short-sleeved shirts
Long-sleeved shirts
Woollen sweater or zip-up fleece
Long cotton trousers
Shorts
Lightweight waterproof jacket
Windproof jacket
Waterproof overtrousers
Walking boots
Spare boot laces
Lightweight trainers or flip-flops
Swimwear
Sturdy belt
Fleece or woollen gloves
Fleece or woollen hat
Wide-brimmed sunhat
Sunglasses
Towelling sweat rag or head scarf
Set of smart clothing plus suitable
    footwear
Nightwear

### Personal equipment
Compass
Maps
Wristwatch
Water bottle and case
Whistle
Cotton money belt
Kitbag or backpack
Day sack
Tent
Sleeping bag
Sleeping mat
Small stuff sacks and garbage bags
Penknife
Flashlight and spare batteries
2 x plates or set of army mess tins
Mug
Knife, fork, spoon
Dishtowel
Pan scourer

Can opener
Travel wash or soap flakes
Clothes pegs (pins)
4m/13ft washline
Small folding camp chair
Walking poles

### Wash kit
Towel
Soap
Toothbrush
Toothpaste
Steel mirror
Hairbrush or comb
Shampoo
Sanitary protection
Razor and shaving foam
Lipbalm
Deodorizing foot powder
Zinc and castor oil cream
Sunscreen
Insect repellent
Pocket tissues
Wet wipes
Washbasin plug

### Miscellaneous items
Passport
Travel tickets
Cash, travellers' cheques, credit card
Vaccination certificate
Repair kit
Camera, spare batteries and film
Mobile (cell) phone
Binoculars
2 x spare passport photos
Photocopies of paperwork
Notebook, pen and pencil

### Personal first-aid kit
Adhesive dressings (plasters),
    various sizes
Paracetamol tablets
Blister kit
Travel sickness tablets
Sterile dressings, various sizes
Triangular bandage
Roller bandages
Small pair of scissors
Thermometer
Tweezers
Safety pins
Disposable gloves

For more extreme weather conditions, add the following items:

### Hot climate extras
Personal water purifier
Malaria tablets
Insect repellent bands and head net
Mosquito net and frame
Camp bed or hammock
Cotton liner for sleeping bag
Shade sheet
Machete
Extra water bottle

### Cold climate/snow extras
Thermal underwear
Down or fleece zip-up jacket
Water- and windproof jacket and
    overtrousers, or fibre-pile
    one-piece suit
Balaclava
Inner or liner gloves
Fleece or woollen mitts
Outer mitts
Knee-length gaiters
Snow shoes or snow boots
Crampons
Climbing harness
Ice axe
Bivvy bag
Space blanket

For trips involving paddling or cycling activities, add the following items:

### Kayaking or canoeing extras
Boat and paddles
Buoyancy aid or Personal flotation
    device (PDF)
Helmet
Thermal or cotton T-shirt
Thermal or cotton trousers
Cagoule and waterproof trousers
Technical sandals, lightweight trainers
    or neoprene boots
Spraydeck (spray skirt) (kayaks only)
Waterproof kit bags and containers

### Cycling extras
Cycle
Helmet
Gloves
Lightweight trainers

# Personal Camp Kit

There are several core items of equipment that you will need to complete ordinary daily tasks while you are away. These items are known as your personal camp kit. You may feel that some of the items listed here are not relevant for your trip, and there may be other items you do need, but this list makes an excellent starting point when you first begin to pack.

### WATER BOTTLE
Drinking water is essential for survival, and when travelling in the wilderness you will need to carry all the water required between water sources. Buy good quality water bottles because you risk serious problems if your bottle leaks and you lose all your supply when you are a long way from a water source. Bottles are available in a range of sizes: quart/pint sizes are the most useful because they are not too heavy to carry when full. An attached bottle cap is best because it cannot get lost; caps that you drink through are very prone to leakages.

### WATER PURIFIER
These are widely available from outdoor suppliers, and you will need to carry one if you are travelling in an area where the purity of the drinking water is in doubt. Fill the bottles with water and leave for 15 minutes, then pour the water through the bottle cap, which acts as a sterilizing filter. The filtered water will be fit to drink.

### MONEY
While travelling keep your cash and your passport in a cotton money belt, strapped under your clothing so that it is out of view but still readily accessible. As insurance, keep an emergency fund of low denomination bills in a separate part of the belt from your main money.

Your choice of currency will depend where you are travelling to, but also remember to carry currency for any countries you will be passing through on the way to your final destination. If travelling to parts of the developing world with a minor local currency that is not available in your own country, a supply of US dollars can be extremely useful. Take around US$100 in $10 and $1 bills. US dollars are accepted in most parts of the world.

### COMPASS AND MAPS
If you are travelling to a remote area or backpacking, it is essential for each person to have their own compass and be able to use it correctly. Keep it near to hand, either in a buttoned-up pocket, or on a strong cord around your neck. A good map is also essential in the wilderness, but it will only be useful if you know how to read it. A planimetric map shows road systems and towns and is a useful for planning your transport route, but to learn about the shape of the land you need a topographic map. This is essential for any walking trip.

### WASH KIT AND TOWEL
Besides soap, toothbrush and toothpaste, facecloth and hairbrush or comb, your camp wash kit should include shampoo, a nail brush, a pair of nail scissors, and a razor and shaving foam if needed. This should be stored in a compact waterproof bag. Take both a bath and a hand towel. A supply of flat-packed toilet tissue is a good idea. Women may prefer to take sanitary protection items with them as they may be hard to find in a remote area or expensive.

◄ *Impure water is poured into the filter of this water purifier and pure water drips into the bottle below.*

### FIRST AID KIT
Include a basic first-aid kit containing waterproof plasters in various sizes, some sterile gauze wound dressings, medication for diarrhoea, aspirin or paracetamol (acetaminophen), indigestion tablets and a few sachets of rehydration powder.

### BATTERIES
Unless you are sure you will be able to buy them while you are away, carry plenty of spare batteries for use in electrical items, such as torches and radios. Include both alkaline and lithium batteries in your kit. Alkaline batteries cost less than lithium batteries and they are more widely available, but lithium batteries run for longer and can be used in much colder temperatures. Dispose of used batteries with care. Do not burn them or bury them in the ground because the iron they contain can leach out into the earth; take them with you or dispose of them in a garbage bin.

### WRISTWATCH
It is tempting to do away with the trappings of urban life when in the wilderness, but you should always wear an accurate wristwatch. Besides showing the time a watch can be used as a simple check that you are on course on your route. When travelling check

▼ *Use a wristwatch set to local time to check you are where you expected to be on your route and to measure travel speeds.*

► *Choose a flashlight that is as small as possible and waterproof as part of your kit.*

◄ *A Swiss Army penknife is compact and includes some valuable features.*

the time when you reach scheduled rest points to make sure you are in line with the day's plan; if you haven't reached a checkpoint by a certain time, it could be an indication that you have taken a wrong turning.

### FLASHLIGHT

A small hand-held flashlight is useful for inside the tent or to read a map in dim light or darkness. If you have the space in your pack, take a head torch as well, as this will allow you to work with your hands free – if you have to put up a tent or change a cycle tyre in the dark, for example, or in an emergency situation at night.

### EATING EQUIPMENT

Take two plates, one of which should be a deep bowl type, or a set of army mess tins. The advantage of the latter is that you can use them for cooking as well as eating. You will also need a mug (about 300ml/½ pint capacity). Consider the pros and cons of plastic equipment versus enamel and aluminium. Plastic is light and less likely to burn you if filled with hot food or liquid, but it can melt if left

too near to a direct heat source. On the other hand, enamel and aluminium are hardwearing, but they are heavier than plastic and can get very hot when filled with hot food or liquid. Your knife, fork and spoon should be made of aluminium or toughened plastic. Buy special camping cutlery if you can as it will be lighter and less bulky than kitchen cutlery.

### PENKNIFE

If you do not have the space for a comprehensive tool kit, a good penknife such as the Swiss Army knife can be almost as useful. Carry it in your main kit bag before a flight (you will not be able to travel on a plane with a penknife in your hand luggage), then transfer it to your person when you arrive.

### CLOTHES WASHING KIT

A small amount of detergent, a washing line and some clothes pegs are handy to wash clothing while at camp.

### REPAIR KITS

A mending kit can be as small as a matchbox but it should contain thread and needles and one or two spare buttons of different sizes, plus a few saftey pins and a small pair of scissors. Lightweight compact repair kits are widely available from outdoor suppliers.

### ELECTRONIC EQUIPMENT

A radio is not essential, but it can help to make longer trips more enjoyable. Other gadgets you may want to take include a camera and

◄ *Each person will need their own mug, bowl, plate and cutlery. Sturdy plastic equipment will avoid mouth burns from hot food.*

a mobile (cell) phone and charger. If travelling abroad you will also need to take an adapter.

### SLEEPING BAG AND MAT

Choose a sleeping bag that is suited to the climate because otherwise you will spend your nights too warm or too cold, and in extreme conditions this could be dangerous. You can also carry an insulated sleeping mat to put underneath your sleeping bag. The bag provides your home comforts while you are living outdoors, so look after it well and do not allow it to get wet. If it does, make it a priority to dry it out as soon as you can. For more information, *see the section on* Sleeping Bags.

▲ *Your sleeping bag should be stored properly when not in use and you should not allow it to get wet.*

### TRAVEL GAMES

A selection of games will provide entertainment in the evenings or on rest days. If you're staying in one location you can take several board games as well as bat and ball games, but if weight and bulk are a problem a pack of playing cards will fit into a pocket.

### WRITING MATERIALS

A notebook and pencil are useful for writing notes for people or for keeping a journal or log of your trip. Remember to keep paper in a plastic bag to protect it from getting damp.

# Basic Survival Kit

If you are travelling in the wilderness it is highly advisable to carry a survival kit. The purpose of the kit is to keep you alive for 24–72 hours if you find yourself lost or injured without shelter, fire or water. It can quite literally mean the difference between life and death.

The survival kit must be carried on your person at all times to be sure it is there when you need it, so keep it small and light; attaching it to a sturdy belt around the waist is ideal. The contents should not be used for any other reason. It should be checked often and items replaced as necessary. Keep the kit in a waterproof pouch bag or in a small tin with a tight-fitting lid.

Your priority in a crisis will be to:
• Protect yourself from the elements
• Make a fire
• Carry and purify water to drink
• Signal your position
• Find your way
• Perform simple first aid

It is important to practise basic survival skills using the equipment in your kit, so that you will know what to do if a situation does arise.

**MAKING A SHELTER**
Your first priority in a survival situation is to construct a shelter for warmth and to give you a refuge while you take stock of your position.

### Space blanket
A lightweight blanket, known as a space blanket, can be used in three ways: to keep warm, with the reflective silver material preventing body heat from escaping and deflecting it back to the body; as a horizontal shelter to reflect the sun's heat away from you; and as an A-shaped shelter to keep you dry from rain.

▲ A space blanket helps to retain body heat and can be used to deflect the sun's rays away from you.

◀ The orange-coloured bivvy bag is light, packs up small and can be a lifesaver in several different ways.

▶ Keep your survival kit small enough to carry on your person.

Notepaper

Pencil

Space blanket

Wind- and waterproof matches

Bivvy bag

Waterproof pouch bag

Potassium permanganate

Sterile wipes and plasters

Water-sterilizing tablets

Sterile wound dressing

Flint and steel

Whistle

Compass

Heavy-duty twine

Wire saw

Fishing wire and tin opener

### Bivvy bag

A large orange-coloured body-size heavy-duty plastic bag, known as a bivvy bag, has many uses yet is very light to carry. You can get into the bag as a way of keeping warm in cold and windy conditions; for a case of hypothermia, while you are waiting for help to arrive, one person can get inside the bag along with the casualty, using the body as an effective heat source to keep the casualty warm. In addition, the bivvy bag can be used as a groundsheet, or it can be used to signal to the air rescue services in an emergency situation: the bright orange colour makes it highly visible from the air, even in severe weather conditions.

▼ *A length of sturdy cord should be included as part of your main kit.*

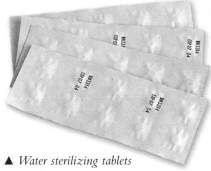

▲ *Water sterilizing tablets are a vital part of your survival kit.*

### Cord

If you need to construct a shelter, you will find parachute cord useful. Carry about 20m/66ft of the cord, packed inside your survival bag.

### Wire saw

This packs up very small and is very effective for cutting through small to medium-size tree branches if you need to make a shelter or cut fire wood.

### LIGHTING A FIRE

You can buy ready-to-use fire-making kits, or you can make your own. A flint and steel is the most effective homemade version, or you can carry a small amount of cotton wool, in case you cannot find kindling, and a small magnifying lens for starting a fire from the sun, a disposable lighter and waterproofed matches (lifeboat matches, which burn in high wind and when wet, are the best). If using matches, keep the striking surface dry and carry an extra striking surface in your survival kit.

### Candles

Tealight candles will take up very little room in your pack and can be used to light fires. Do not carry tallow candles as they will melt in hot weather.

### CARRYING AND CLEANING WATER

Once you have found a source of water, you need a container to carry it in. A plastic bag or a condom can be used for this purpose; a condom can hold over 9 litres/2 gallons of water. Put the condom full of water into a sock or knotted trouser leg for added strength and protection. Before drinking the water, you will need to purify it using water-sterilizing tablets. Include a small phial of potassium permanganate, which can also be used to purify water (it is also an antiseptic and can be used to light a campfire). For more information, see the section Clean Water.

► *Tealight candles burn easily and can be used to light a fire.*

► *Firelighting kits, available from outdoor suppliers, contain flint and steel, tinder and matches.*

### SIGNALLING

Pack a small flashlight and a heliograph, and wear a whistle on a cord around your neck. A few sheets of paper and a pencil will allow you to leave messages for rescuers trying to track you. A bivvy bag will enable you to signal your location.

### FINDING YOUR WAY

Carry a spare compass in your survival kit as back-up in case you lose or damage your first compass.

### FIRST-AID KIT

The survival kit should include the following first aid items:
- Adhesive dressings (plasters)
- Sterile wound dressing
- Sachets of rehydration powder
- Salt tablets
- Crêpe bandage
- Sterile scalpel blade
- Darning needle
- Length of thread or wool

### FOOD

Your body can last for up to five days without food, whereas it will last only 24 hours without water. This makes eating your least immediate need in a survival situation. Including food in your kit is not practical but if you carry a length of fishing wire and plenty of fish hooks and sinkers you will be equipped to catch fish for eating.

► *Learn how to use fishing wire, hooks and weights for catching fish.*

# Choosing a Tent

When you choose a tent, you will be faced with a huge selection of styles, colours, weights and sizes. To help narrow down your choice, and to make sure you end up buying what you do actually need, consider where and when you are going to use the tent, how you are going to carry it, what you are going to use it for and how many people it will need to sleep.

### WHERE AND WHEN ARE YOU GOING TO USE THE TENT?
Consider the climate you can expect at your destination and the environment in which you are going to camp. In the African bush your tent will need to protect you from the heat and possibly from heavy rain; on a mountainside above the Arctic Circle your priority is protection from high winds.

▲ *Small robust tents are preferable for use in exposed sites or colder climates, with the lower volume of air space retaining the heat.*

▼ *In hot, dry climates choose a larger tent with more internal space that encourages air circulation and keeps the temperature down.*

▲ *The general-purpose ridge tent is suitable for climatic conditions anywhere in the world, and is available in a range of sizes.*

▲ *Some vehicles have been adapted to take a tent on the roof to give protection from wild animals attracted to the camp at night.*

▲ *A contemporary one-person tunnel tent. The hoop pole structure offers good floor space but will not withstand high winds.*

If you are going to a hot, dry climate try to allow for as much space in your tent as possible to encourage the air to circulate and keep you cooler. If you are backpacking you will need to consider the pros and cons of an airy tent against the extra bulk to be carried. Cotton and canvas materials will stand up to and protect you from the sun far better than synthetic materials. Strong ultraviolet light in the tropics can ruin nylon materials very quickly, and the thorns on many bushes and trees can destroy lightweight material.

### TENT CRITERIA

The tent is your home while you are in the wilderness. Its main function is to provide a warm and dry place for you to sleep, but you may also need to cook inside it or use it as a shelter while you sit out severe weather conditions. The following criteria are essential:
- The tent should be big enough to allow sleeping space and adequate ventilation for all users and their kit.
- There should be enough height on the inside for everyone to sit upright at the same time.
- The flooring material needs to be robust enough to give protection from the ground; if it isn't you will need to carry additional matting if you are to sleep in comfort.

If the climate is hot and wet, and you visit in the rainy season, the tent may have to withstand weeks or months of heavy rain. Natural materials such as cotton or canvas will cope better with this type of climate.

In high mountains in a cold climate, you will want a small tent that will warm up quickly with your body heat and will be able to withstand high winds. A tent made from synthetic materials will be lighter, and therefore easier to carry, than a cotton or canvas one. It will also be stronger, with a sewn-in groundsheet, made of a substantial material, suitable for pitching on snow, ice and rocks.

In very extreme cold conditions you may find that the tent doors are better fastened by some other means than a zip, such as tied or velcro fasteners, because zips can freeze if it is extremely cold.

### HOW ARE YOU GOING TO CARRY THE TENT?

If you plan to transport your tent in the back of a vehicle, then weight or size will not be a major consideration. However, if you will be carrying the tent yourself, you will need to choose the lightest option possible (see the section Lightweight Camping).

▶ *The geodesic dome tent is spacious on the inside, and if the sloping wall is pitched in the direction of the wind it is very stable.*

### WHAT ARE YOU GOING TO USE THE TENT FOR?

Is your tent going to be used for backpacking, where you will set it up for the night, cook, sleep, then take it down and move on? Or are you going to set up camp and use your tent as a work place, eating, sleeping and general living area, perhaps staying for several days or weeks? Think about how you will use the tent and choose accordingly.

### HOW MANY PEOPLE WILL THE TENT NEED TO SLEEP?

If your tent is going to be used in a base camp, decide how many people it will need to sleep, and how much room you will allow each person. If you have a mixed-sex group, they may prefer to be separated for sleeping, using either a divided tent or separate smaller tents. How much kit each person will have must also be taken into account if the kit is going to be stored inside the tent.

## RIDGE TENT

This general-purpose tent is suitable for camping anywhere, from the back garden to the desert or jungle. The ridge tent has an upright pole or an A-shaped pole assembly at each end, and, in some cases, an additional ridgepole across the top. This adds extra weight but it also stabilizes the tent, and this could be important if you are likely to experience high winds. Some ridge tents have sloping ridges to cut down on weight.

The walls of the ridge tent are created by adjustable guy lines, which stretch the inner walls outwards,

### KEY QUESTIONS

Before making any decisions, look at the styles available and talk to a reputable tent retailer before asking yourself the following questions:

- How heavy is the tent? Pick up a packed version to feel the weight for yourself.
- Are there additional features that are of no use but add to the cost?
- Is the stitching well done and are the guying and guy line points reinforced to take the strain?
- Are the poles strong enough for the job and would they support the material in strong winds?
- If the tent gets damaged in the field, can it be repaired quickly and easily?
- If it is a dome tent can you buy spare poles for it?
- How easy is it to pitch the tent, not just on a summer's day in a local field but also on a mountain in high winds in near darkness?
- How many people are required to pitch the tent?
- Is the tent material of good quality and will it stand up well to the conditions you are going to take it into?
- Will you need a two-skin tent, i.e. an inner tent with a fly sheet, and will the fly sheet need to come right down to the ground to offer you protection in wet and windy conditions?

supporting the tent and allowing you to utilize the whole of the floor space without touching the sides of the tent. This is important because if the inner walls touch the outer fly sheet and the fly sheet is wet, the dampness will soak through to the inner walls, causing water to leach inside the tent. A door at each end is the preferred choice, so that if you have to cook in a doorway due to intense cold or heavy rain you can choose the door opening that offers the most shelter from the prevailing wind and the elements.

▲ *A standard ridge tent is simple to erect and maintain even for most inexperienced campers, hence its continued popularity.*

## BELL OR SINGLE-POLE TENTS

Bell tents have a single pole in the middle of the tent, while single-pole tents may have either a pole or an A-shaped pole assembly. Both designs are very stable in strong winds.

▼ *Large patrol tents are ideal for basecamps but the size and weight of the canvas means they will have to be transported by vehicle.*

## DOME AND GEODESIC DOME TENTS

These have a number of poles threaded into sleeves on either the inner or outer tent. The extra poles make these the most expensive types of tent to buy, and if your poles break you will need spares or splints to slide over the break.

The geodesic dome is more stable than the ordinary dome in bad weather, but it is difficult to pitch in high winds.

## TUNNEL AND WEDGE TENTS

The tunnel tent is a cross between a ridge tent and a dome. It offers good floor space as the pole system is a series of hoops down the tent, but in high winds it can blow in and lose its shape. The wedge tent has most of the disadvantages of the tunnel and few advantages. Instability is a problem in bad weather as the large areas of material are a target for high winds.

▲ *Wedge and tunnel tents on display at an outdoor suppliers fair. The advantages of these tents are their small size and low weight, making them popular with backpackers. One disadvantage is the lack of headroom.*

▼ *Geodesic dome tents are one of the sturdiest tents available and will withstand even gale-force winds so long as the poles – which are threaded through the fabric to give the tent its shape – are not damaged.*

▼ *Large frame tents provide useful areas for study or group meetings at base camps, but several people will be needed to put them up.*

# Sleeping Bags

A comfortable, warm sleeping bag will give you the good night's sleep you need when living outdoors. Getting enough sleep is as important to your physical health and state of mind as eating, and the right bag is important.

All sleeping bags work by trapping air in their fillings; the air is warmed by the heat from your body and retained in the filling, insulating you against the cold. The more warm air a bag traps, the greater its insulating properties.

There is a huge variety of sleeping bags available, from inexpensive but basic simple-quilted versions to quality, down-filled double-quilted ones. The criteria to look for when choosing a bag are the method of construction, what material is used, what filling is used, how it is zipped, its size and whether or not it has a hood.

## CONSTRUCTION

There are basically three different types of sleeping bag construction: simple quilting or stitch-through; box-wall; and double quilting.

### Simple quilting or stitch-through

This method is usually used in the cheaper sleeping bags. They are not very effective at retaining warmth because warm air will be lost where the stitching goes through the fabric. These bags have a low temperature rating, making them suitable for warm summer weather, or for two consecutive seasons: spring and summer or summer and autumn.

### Box-wall

Bags with this type of construction have a high temperature rating, and they may be suitable for two to three seasons, or even three to four seasons in a temperate climate. They come in three different forms.
- Box-wall construction, where the filling is contained within "boxes" to prevent the filling from moving about.
- Slant-wall construction, with slanted layers of overlapping fibres. This improves on the box-wall version by giving the filling more room to expand, filling with air for improved insulation and, therefore, warmth.
- V-baffle construction, which improves on the slant-wall construction by making sure there is always plenty of filling throughout the bag.

### Double quilting

This is effectively two simple quilting or stitch-through-type sleeping bags put together and offset to eliminate cold spots. It usually has the highest-quality filling but is heavy to carry and may not be suitable for backpacking trips.

## MATERIAL

Your choice of material for the shell depends on the type of environment and what time of year you will be using the sleeping bag:
- Cotton is ideally suited to high temperatures and humidity as it is a breathable natural fabric and will absorb sweat and feel comfortable.

**WARMTH RATINGS**

Consider any kind of sleeping bag rating as a rough guide only as there is no standard rating system. Some manufacturers describe the number of seasons a bag may be suitable for. Others give temperature ranges; these may be the range of temperature in which the bag will feel comfortably warm, or it may be the temperature at which you will survive but won't feel warm.

- Nylon is better suited to cooler temperatures, where sweating is not likely to be a problem; some nylon sleeping bags have a cotton lining on the inside, which increases the comfort factor.
- Pertex is a good down-proofing material, which means that it stops the filling material from working its way through the fabric. It is also water-repellent (but not water*proof*), which makes it suitable for damp, though not wet, conditions, such as high humidity.

Military-type sleeping bags have a groundsheet sewn on to the underneath of the bag so they can be used directly on the ground, even without a tent or sleeping mat. However, these bags are often heavy and bulky and they can be difficult to clean. They are available from specialist outdoor stores that sell ex-military equipment.

▲ *Simple or stitch-through quilting is found in cheaper sleeping bags that are suitable for one or two seasons of the year.*

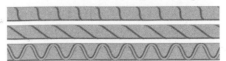

▲ *Box-wall construction comes in three forms: box-wall (top and main diagram), slant-wall (centre) and V-baffle (bottom).*

▲ *Double-quilting construction is effectively two simple or stitch-through bags put together and offset to better retain the heat.*

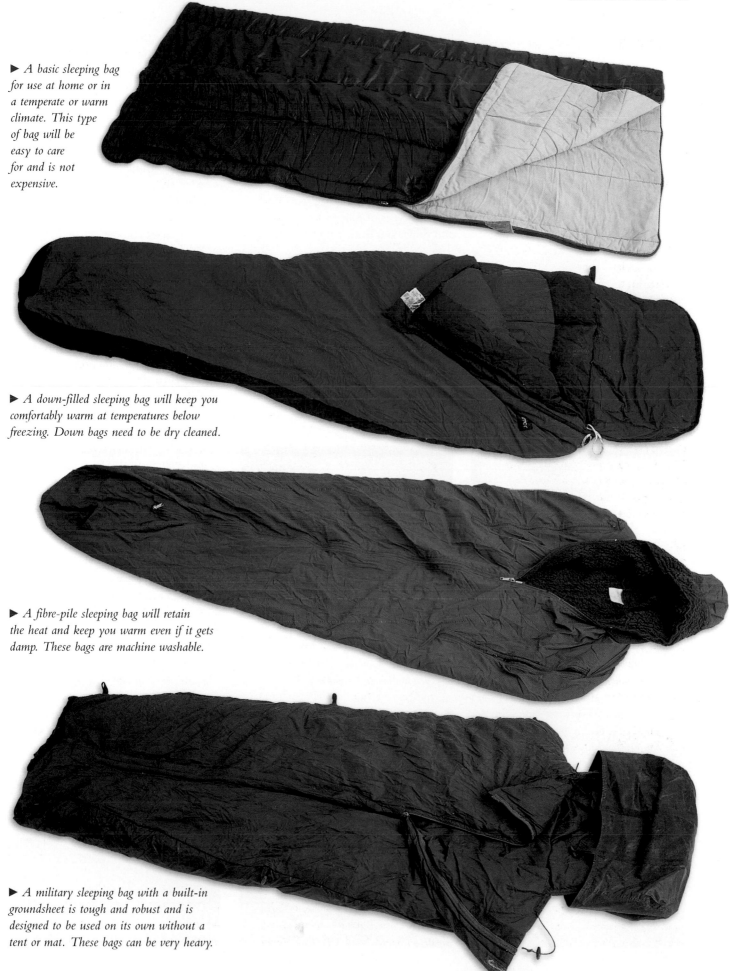

▶ *A basic sleeping bag for use at home or in a temperate or warm climate. This type of bag will be easy to care for and is not expensive.*

▶ *A down-filled sleeping bag will keep you comfortably warm at temperatures below freezing. Down bags need to be dry cleaned.*

▶ *A fibre-pile sleeping bag will retain the heat and keep you warm even if it gets damp. These bags are machine washable.*

▶ *A military sleeping bag with a built-in groundsheet is tough and robust and is designed to be used on its own without a tent or mat. These bags can be very heavy.*

## FACTORS AFFECTING WARMTH

How warm your sleeping bag will keep you is dependent on a number of variable factors besides bag construction and filling:

- The climate, including the humidity level (high humidity makes the bag damp, and increases heat loss through conduction).
- Whether you are in a tent or shelter, or out in the open air.
- Whether you are on your own inside the sleeping bag.
- Whether or not you are using a sleeping mat underneath the bag.
- What clothes you are wearing.
- The shape of the bag, with a close-fitting bag being warmer.
- How much you have eaten, as food provides energy and heat.
- How tired you are, as it is more difficult to get warm when tired.

## FILLINGS

The biggest difference between bags is in the type of filling and the thickness of it. The purpose of a sleeping bag filling is to trap air as insulation. The thicker the filling, and the more effectively it traps the air, the better the bag will be at keeping you warm.

### Natural fillings

Feather-filled sleeping bags have one of three types of filling: down, feather, and down and feather mix.

### Down

Pure down is the fluffy underplumage of ducks and/or geese. It is by far the lightest and warmest, weight for weight, of all bag fillings, and is comfortable over a greater temperature range. Down shapes itself around the body for a close, warm fit, unlike synthetic fillings, which tend to stand away from the body, leaving cold spots. Down is more compressible than synthetic fillings, so it packs up much smaller and won't get damaged when stuffed into a rucksack. The drawbacks of down are that it loses its insulation properties when wet, and takes a long time to dry out. It can also be damaged by damp storage. However, it is difficult to get a down bag wet in the first place, unless you drop it in water or sleep outside in the rain without shelter. This is especially so with modern shell materials, which are water-resistant and dry out quickly.

Although down bags are expensive, they can be expected to last much longer than synthetic bags – for up to 20 years if well cared for – and this makes them a more economical choice in the long term. They are most suitable for situations where warmth and space are at a premium, and are a particular favourite for cold conditions because of their comfort, weight and bulk.

### Down/feather mix

A number of manufacturers mix duck or goose down and feathers together to make a cheaper filling (separating the feathers from the stalkless down plumules is very time-consuming and therefore expensive). The mixed filling has all the advantages of down: it is warm and comfortable, light to carry and easily packed up, although you do need more filling to achieve the same level of warmth. Check what proportion of down makes up the filling, as a greater amount of down means a warmer sleeping bag. There will usually be less than 50 per cent down in the mix.

▲ *A fibre-pile filling will keep you warm even if it becomes damp or wet, and this may be crucial in a cold and wet climate.*

▲ *Synthetic bag fillings are cheaper than down and although they weigh more, they will perform better when damp or wet.*

▼ *Duck or goose down is the most costly bag filling but it is also the most effective at retaining heat and it will last the longest.*

▼ *Feather filling uses poorer quality feathers than down and requires more in weight and bulk to provide the same amount of heat.*

▼ *Many people find a down and feather mix a good compromise between cost and the ability to insulate effectively.*

▲ *At good outdoor suppliers you will be faced with a huge selection of sleeping bags. Always ask for advice if you feel confused.*

### Feather

These are the bigger, stiffer feathers of ducks and geese, which you will be able to feel through the bag shell. A feather filling will not have the same insulation properties as down or the down/feather mix, and you will need at least twice as much filling to achieve the same warmth, but feather bags are less expensive and they can still provide a very comfortable night's sleep.

### Synthetic fillings

These fillings don't have the natural lightness of down or feather fillings, and synthetic bags at the cheaper end of the market tend to be heavy, bulky and less soft. They are also less durable, as the synthetic filling starts to lose its insulation properties after only a couple of years. However, synthetic bags are inexpensive to buy. They perform well when wet and dry out quickly, and are machine washable. They are more tolerant of careless handling and damp conditions than down bags, and are perfectly adequate for situations where warmth, low weight and bulk are not your priority.

One specialist synthetic filling is fibre pile, which is a thicker version of the material used for fleece jackets. Fibre pile will retain its insulation properties when wet, it can be hung out to dry, and is machine washable. However, it is bulkier and heavier than other synthetic-filled bags, and it may not be suitable for lightweight camping. Fibre-pile fillings can be difficult to find in stores.

### SIZE AND SHAPE

Try out the bag in the store to see if it is wide and long enough for you. A bag that fits close to your body will keep you warmer than a roomy one, but check it doesn't feel too restrictive. Better quality bags have a tapered shape.

### ZIPS

Most bags have a zip of some kind to allow the bag to be opened out full, which makes getting in and out easy, and allows for ventilation. It is also useful for cleaning the bag. Zips can be full-length, half-length, or down one side and across the bottom. Any zip is a potential cold spot, though a quality bag will have a protected pad of filling under the zip. If a bag does not have a zip, it will be more difficult to get into but will weigh less.

### HOOD

Some 20 per cent of body heat is lost through the head, and a bag with a hood retains warmth more effectively. It also makes a comfortable resting place for your head, and can be pulled up over your head to protect you from insects, such as flies or mosquitos.

### SAFETY

Never leave your sleeping bag or liner on the ground for any length of time, even when it is rolled up, but pack it away in your rucksack. In temperate or hot countries, unroll your sleeping bag only just before you get into it to avoid any insects getting in with you.

▼ *Sleeping out without a tent can be great fun but do not sleep too near the camp fire or else you could damage your sleeping bag.*

# Other Sleeping Equipment

Additional items can be added to your kit for a more comfortable night's sleep. Consider the cost of buying and transporting these extra items, as well as the additional weight and bulk if you are backpacking and have to carry them.

**INSULATION AND PROTECTION**
You may want to insulate yourself from the ground if it will be cold, hard or wet, or if there will be ants, snakes or spiders on it.

### Camp beds
These come in all shapes and sizes and are heavy, so you will want to use them only if transporting your equipment by vehicle or pack animal. However, camp beds will get you right off the ground for a very comfortable night's sleep.

If you are going to use a camp bed, you will need some insulation beneath the sleeping bag, such as a mat, as the layer of air between you and the ground will become very cold at night. If you are going to an area where there will be mosquitos, consider setting up a frame around your bed for a mosquito net. When using a camp bed, always set it up on flat ground, so that you don't tip the bed over accidentally when turning over in the night.

### Air mattresses
These require inflating by mouth or with an air pump, and this makes them time-consuming to set up. Air mattresses come in different sizes, colours and thicknesses. If over-inflated, they may feel hard and uncomfortable to sleep on.

An air mattress full of air becomes cold overnight, so in anything but hot weather, you will need extra insulation underneath you, such as an insulated mat. Be careful that the mattress does not get punctured by sharp stones on the ground or carelessly pierced by a knife or penknife, and do not drag it along the ground; carry a puncture repair kit so that if necessary you can make repairs in the field.

### Self-inflating sleeping mats
When you unscrew the valve on one of these mats, air will be sucked in and it will inflate itself, though you can speed up the process by giving one or two puffs of air by mouth to start off with. Check for sharp stones or thorns on the ground before laying the mat out. These mats are best carried inside the rucksack to protect them from damage.

### Insulation mats
These are the lightest and cheapest type of insulation, and they come in several thicknesses. If you are going to a very cold climate, a thick foam mat will provide good insulation but it will be heavy to carry and bulky. The great advantage with these mats is that you cannot damage them, except by putting them in direct contact with something

◄ *Metal frame camp beds are bulky and heavy but they do keep you off the ground and this will greatly improve your comfort.*

▼ *Insulation mats are available in a range of thicknesses and lengths, so choose one for the conditions you will be sleeping in.*

▼ *Self-inflating mats are convenient to use, but do not over-inflate them and watch for sharp stones or rocks on the ground beneath.*

▼ *A cotton sleeping bag liner will help to keep the sleeping bag clean and is easy to wash.*

▲ *A mosquito net is essential for tropical climates. Attach it to the inside of your tent and check daily for tears.*

▶ *Self-inflating sleeping mats can be rolled up neatly and strapped on to the outside of your rucksack during transit.*

▼ *An inflatable pillow is small and light enough even for backpackers to carry, and will improve your night-time comfort.*

very hot, which will melt them. Check for stones on the ground when you unroll your mat, which could give you an uncomfortable night's sleep.

### NEWSPAPER

If you are lightweight camping without a sleeping mat, and are going to have to sleep on the ground with only the tent groundsheet for insulation, you can lay sheets of newspaper under your sleeping bag. You will need at least five to ten sheets of newspaper for effective insulation, but it is better than nothing if the ground is very cold or hard.

### SLEEPING BAG LINERS

Whichever material you choose for the outer shell of your sleeping bag, you might want to consider buying a separate liner. This is a thin fabric bag, usually made of cotton or silk, which fits inside the sleeping bag. It does offer a little more warmth, but its main advantage is that it protects the sleeping bag from getting dirty on the inside,

and it can be washed more easily than the bag. In hot weather, you can sleep in the liner on its own, perhaps using your sleeping bag underneath it for padding, as you would a sleeping mat.

### INFLATABLE PILLOW

Although it is not strictly necessary, an inflatable pillow weighs next to nothing and will add to your comfort during the night. It can also be used to give head and neck support on long journeys. Inflate the pillow by mouth at your campsite and deflate it after use, so that it can be folded up and packed with your tent bag or tucked into your rucksack.

# Backpacks and Carrying Equipment

A backpack is used to carry food and clothing while on the move. It can be used to carry camping and cooking gear if you will be living outdoors and without any other means of transporting your gear. The backpack you need for a day's walking in warm weather will be very different to the one needed for a three-week camping trip through the mountains. As with any equipment, decide how you will be using the pack before you buy one.

Many modern backpacks are covered in straps, zips, gadgets and pockets, and these additional features will often add to the price. Rather than being dazzled by the apparent complexity of these backpacks, consider if you really need the extra features. Remember, too, that most people will fill whatever size backpack they have, which can make for a very heavy load, so the smaller the sack, the less temptation there will be to take too much gear.

All backpacks are claimed to be waterproof but some fabric materials are better than others, and it is a good idea to line the main compartment with a plastic bag to keep your gear dry. (You may prefer crucial items such as your passport or first-aid kit to be wrapped in additional sturdy plastic bags as a further safeguard.)

## DAY SACKS

For a day's walking in the summer, a small, light day sack with a capacity of between 20 and 35 litres containing food and water, waterproof clothing and emergency supplies will be as much as you need. If your activities will involve mountaineering, ski touring or snow hiking, choose one of the larger day sacks of around 40 litres.

### Additional features

Day sacks do not need a support frame because they are not designed to carry heavy loads. Even so, comfort is always important, and because a day sack sits directly against your back, padding on the outside is advisable so that any sharp contents do not dig into you.

*Main compartment*

*Lockable zip opening to main compartment*

*Smaller front compartment*

*Lockable zip opening to front compartment*

*Document pocket for quick-access items*

*Mesh side pockets*

▲ *A day sack should be big enough to carry your waterproofs and a sweater, a survival kit, and enough food and water for the day.*

In addition, when packing make sure you place soft items such as clothing against the rear of the pack to act as an extra cushion for your back.

In hot weather or during strenuous activities, wearing the sack may cause your back to sweat. To control this, many better-designed packs have a robust cotton panel on the back to absorb sweat; a cotton panel feels more comfortable than a synthetic one. Quality modern sacks are fitted with a high-wicking padded mesh back for improved ventilation to reduce sweating.

Day sacks do not usually have pockets on the outside because the main compartment is small enough to be easily accessible. There will usually be a pocket in the top flap, which is useful for holding maps and valuables.

Larger day sacks will come with a waist strap, and if you think you are going to do a lot of scrambling or steep country work, it is advisable to have one of these, otherwise the pack can move around as you climb, and this may affect your balance.

If you are planning to walk over difficult terrain, or are mountaineering, ski touring or snow hiking, choose a larger day sack with attachment points on the outside, which will allow you to fix on your walking pole, ice axe, skis or crampons, keeping your hands free.

Other features include compressible straps, which can be pulled tight to reduce the volume of an empty sack, a key-ring attachment and a top handle.

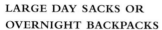

## WHAT TO LOOK FOR IN A PACK

- The pack must be sturdy and comfortable, whatever its size.
- Webbing needs to be tough, in good condition and adjustable. This is especially important on larger packs as heavy loads can quickly weaken poor webbing.
- The outer fabric should be tough and fully waterproof.
- There should be a drawstring hood inside the main sack to prevent water leaking in and contents falling out.
- Outer pockets should have zips rather than straps or drawstrings.
- A comfortable waist belt is essential on any pack bigger than a day sack.

## LARGE DAY SACKS OR OVERNIGHT BACKPACKS

These will come in the 35–55 litre range, and they may have a frame or may be frameless.

As you will be carrying a heavier weight than in a smaller day sack, look closely at the waist or hip belt to see if it is strong and well padded and has a quick-release buckle in case you need to jettison the sack quickly. Also check that the shoulder straps are well padded and that the straps can be tightened or slackened quickly and easily. The webbing on all straps should be well made and strong.

This type of sack can come with external pockets, usually one or two on each side, as well as an easy-access document pocket in the top flap for maps. Side pockets are very useful for keeping water bottles, fuel and other fluids or dirty items of kit away from your main kit to prevent damage in the event of leakage. Make sure zip-up side pockets are kept securely fastened when in use, so that nothing can fall out accidentally.

Whether or not you need a pack with a frame depends on how you will be using the pack and the type of loads you will be carrying. A frame adds extra weight to the pack but it will make heavy or bulky loads more comfortable to carry, and this is very important over long distances.

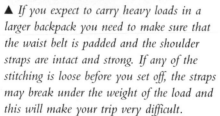

▲ *If you expect to carry heavy loads in a larger backpack you need to make sure that the waist belt is padded and the shoulder straps are intact and strong. If any of the stitching is loose before you set off, the straps may break under the weight of the load and this will make your trip very difficult.*

▲ *If fully packed a large backpack without a frame can cause sweating on the back in hot weather or during strenuous activity.*

▼ *Overnight backpacks will hold equipment for short lightweight camping trips or for day use if work or study gear is to be carried.*

— Elastic holders for easy-access items

— Hooded opening to main compartment

— Front pocket for smaller items

— Zip-fastening side pocket

— Padded waist belt

— Straps to carry equipment externally

# Cooking Stoves

There are five kinds of fuel suitable for outdoor cooking stoves, and all have their advantages and disadvantages, including volatility, smell, ease of use and cost. Which fuel you choose will dictate the type of stove you can take, though multi-fuel stoves, which use more than one type, are available.

When planning your trip, consider the type of conditions you need the stove to operate in. Some gases will not perform well in extreme cold conditions and some fuels evaporate quickly in very hot conditions, so it is important to make a suitable choice. Also note that in some countries you may not be able to buy the right kind of cylinder for your stove.

### GAS
This is probably the most popular and easiest type of stove to use, though the fuel is potentially the most dangerous. There are two types of gas (liquid petroleum gas) available: butane (the more usual) and propane (which will operate in much lower temperatures).

▼ *Gas stoves are available in different sizes but the most important feature for safe use is a stable base to prevent it toppling over.*

◄ *The Trangia stove runs on methylated spirits. It is windproof and stable and includes its own set of cooking pans and a kettle.*

When gas stoves are not being used, they must be turned off and kept in a well-ventilated area, away from sleeping areas. If they do leak, they can build up an invisible layer of gas that can suffocate sleeping people and explode when ignited.

### METHYLATED SPIRITS
The most popular stove of this type is the Trangia stove and cooking set from Sweden, which is windproof and very stable; some models also have a small gas stove attached. These stoves come in two sizes, and each comes with its own set of cooking pans.

Methylated spirits (methyl alcohol) burn very cleanly, but the flame is almost invisible, so great care must be taken when lighting or refilling the burner. It should be carried in a specialized fuel bottle.

### PARAFFIN
This burns in the form of a vapour mixed with air, and it will need to be primed or heated

▲ *A paraffin stove is cheap to run but it can be difficult to use. You may need to practise before taking it into the field for the first time.*

► *A camp oven will allow you to bake fresh bread at a base camp if you are able to transport your gear by vehicle.*

▲ *A petrol stove is versatile and easy to use but can be expensive to buy.*

▲ *A windshield can be fitted around a petrol stove to protect the flame and make cooking more efficient in windy weather.*

### CARRYING SPARE FUEL

Make sure you have an adequate supply of fuel for your cooking stove. If you are travelling abroad you will need to check that the fuel for your stove is available in the country you are going to. If not, you may have to change the type of stove you are using, since most airlines, including all in Europe and the United States, do not allow gas or flammable liquids to be carried on planes.

▼ *Use sturdy metal containers for carrying petrol or paraffin supplies to your destination; use plastic containers for water only.*

with another fuel to bring it to the temperature where it will vaporize. Spilt paraffin will not evaporate and will leave an unpleasant smell. Always store it in a metal fuel bottle in case of leakages.

This kind of stove is cheap to run and burns well with a hot flame, but it is also the most complicated to use and can take a while to get used to. As a further disadvantage it will blacken cooking pans and clog burner jets.

### PETROL

This burns in the form of vapour under pressure and will burn cleanly unless additives are in the fuel. Unlike paraffin, it does not need a secondary fuel to heat it to the required temperature.

Petrol is very volatile and the smell is strong and unpleasant. It must be stored in a special metal fuel container in case of leakages. If spilled it will evaporate quickly, especially if the weather is hot, and it will ruin food and stain fabrics if it comes into contact with them.

### SOLID FUEL

This is available in two forms: tablet (Hexamine) and alcohol jelly. This type of fuel gives off strong and unpleasant fumes, and the flame is difficult to put out (although this can be an advantage in windy conditions) and hard to regulate. Solid fuel stoves must only ever be used in a well-ventilated place.

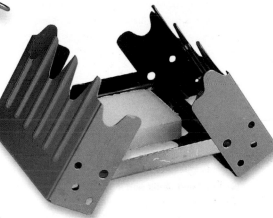

▲ *Solid fuel stoves were first designed to be used by the army. They are for one-time use only but are useful to carry in an emergency.*

### WARNING

All stoves must be treated with care. When lit they use oxygen and give out lethal carbon monoxide, and must be used in a well-ventilated place. Make sure the flame is really out before filling a stove with fuel.

▼ *Solid fuel stoves were first designed for the army. They are now available to the public and are excellent for use in windy conditions.*

# Cooking Equipment

What you need in the way of cooking equipment for a backpacking trip will be minimal, since the priority is to keep your pack weight down and the meals you eat will be basic. At a base or standing camp, you may have the capacity to set up a kitchen to feed a large number of people, who may be ready for better and more varied meals than they have had out in the field. This will require the type of cooking equipment used by a catering kitchen. For anything in between, the sort of equipment you take will depend on how easily you can transport it.

### LIGHTWEIGHT CAMPING
When you are carrying your equipment on your back, you cannot afford to take more than what is essential. While the food you eat is important, its primary function is as a source of energy, and it is unlikely that you will eat as well

▼ *Individuals should carry their own set of cutlery. The advantage of folding sets is that they are very convenient to pack.*

as you would like to. The typical menu will consist of canned, pouch or dehydrated foods, which require little in the way of cooking except to be heated through. A set of mess tins is a practical choice for your equipment because the two tins can be used for both cooking and eating, and can be neatly packed, one inside the other, for storage. A folding aluminium cutlery set takes up little space and will double up as a set of cooking utensils. If you are taking canned foods you need to pack a can opener. Good penknives, such as the Swiss Army knife, can be used as improvised kitchen utensils. The tiny scissors and can opener on the knife will be useful, especially for overnight or ultra-lightweight camping, but for longer trips, a standard household can opener will be easier to use.

### BASE CAMPS
Much more sophisticated meals can be cooked at a base camp, which may stand for several weeks while the team completes a schedule of activities or a course of study. Because a base camp is more permanent, and is not being dismantled and moved on a daily basis, it can be better equipped, with a wider range of sturdy cooking equipment and utensils. You will need to decide the kind of heat source you will be using before choosing your equipment.

### COOKING POTS
Depending on how many people you are catering for, you will need a number of pots in a range of sizes, with some big enough to boil up to 9–13.5 litres/ 2–3 gallons of water. Make sure that all pots are kept clean both inside and out and that the handles are safe and in good working order. Having lids on the pans will reduce cooking times.

◄ *Mess tins pack away neatly with one tin inside the other. They were designed for army use but are now available to the public.*

How heavy your pots will need to be will depend on whether you are using stoves or fires for cooking; lightweight metal containers can be used on stoves, but should never be used on an open fire (see the sections Cooking over a Fire and Cooking on Stoves). Frying pans, in particular, need to be heavy duty because they are used at such high temperatures.

### WATER CONTAINERS
Lightweight campers cannot carry supplies of water and must source it along the route. However, if weight is not an issue because you are travelling by vehicle to a base or standing camp or to a remote area or through a dry climate, you can carry large quantities of water in dixies. These robust containers, which hold several litres of water, are made of plastic and have a screw-top lid that makes them leak-proof. The flat-sided shape of some designs makes them easy to store at camp or during transit. Fuel can be stored in metal jerry cans, but do not carry water in metal containers.

▼ *When a fire of grass or twigs is lit in the base of a volcana kettle, the heat passes up a tube in the container to heat the water.*

◀ *Camp cookware can include a range of pots of different sizes and even an egg poacher.*

▶ *If you are catering for a group you will need cooking pots that hold large quantities.*

◀ *A pair of oven gloves is invaluable to protect your hands when holding a hot pan handle or lifting the lid of a steaming pot.*

## OVEN GLOVES

If you are handling hot, heavy cooking pots and pans you will need something to protect your hands, especially if you are cooking over an open fire. A couple of pairs of oven gloves should always be kept in the cooking area of the camp.

## MIXING BOWLS

You will need a number of bowls in different sizes for food preparation. Bowls can be either plastic or metal; plastic is lighter to carry but must be kept away from the heat source.

▼ *Your choice of cooking utensils will depend on how much weight and bulk you can carry, and the types of food you will be cooking.*

## MEASURING JUGS

These are available in all sizes, so choose the size appropriate for your needs. In a base camp kitchen catering for a number of people one large jug (pitcher) and several medium- and small-sized jugs will be the most useful.

## CHOPPING BOARDS

Separate plastic boards should be used for raw and cooked vegetables, fish and meat and bread. Ideally, the boards should be colour coded so that they are used exclusively for one type of food, such as red for raw meat, blue for fish, green for vegetables, and so on. This will prevent food contamination, which could spark an outbreak of food poisoning among the group.

◀ *Do not forget to carry a can opener if you will be eating canned foods.*

### OTHER USEFUL ITEMS

If you will be cooking for a large number of people from a base camp kitchen, the following items will make your task a lot easier:

- Wooden spoons in different sizes; do not use chipped wooden spoons as these can carry bacteria.
- Two or three serving spoons.
- A large slotted or draining spoon.
- Sharp knives in a range of different sizes, including some serrated knives. Make sure they are kept sharp. Knives should be kept in the camp kitchen at all times and should never be used for any other purpose.
- A fish slice or metal spatula can be used to take delicate foods, such as fried eggs, out of pans.
- Ladles in different sizes for serving soups and sauces.
- Potato peelers and mashers, which can also be used for other root vegetables, such as carrots.
- A hand-held balloon whisk for mixing powdered sauces or soups into water.
- A catering-size can opener if you need to open catering-size cans.
- Sieves for draining rice, pasta and potatoes and other vegetables.
- Salt, pepper, sugar and sauces such as ketchup and mustard.

# Additional Gear

In addition to major items of gear such as backpacks, tents and cooking equipment, and personal gear such as wash kits, radios and flashlights, there are some items of kit that are not essential but may make your trip easier and more comfortable.

## LAMPS

A small gas lamp is a great advantage at camp when night falls. If you take one, make sure you carry extra mantles and pack the lamp well so you do not accidentally break the glass cover in transit. Like gas stoves, gas lamps cannot be carried on planes, but there are some good candle lanterns on the market and these make an effective alternative. Candle lanterns are not as bright as gas lamps, but you can transport them by plane.

▶ *A gas lamp is more convenient than a flashlight as a night-time light source.*

Never leave a lighted gas or candle lamp unattended in a tent, and do not sleep in a confined space with a gas lamp (even if it is turned off) in case it leaks.

## PILLOW

If you find it difficult to sleep without a pillow for your head, you could improvise by folding your dry clothing into a pillow shape to give you a more comfortable night's sleep, or you can take a cotton pillowcase with you to stuff your clothes into, so that your pillow will not disintegrate during the night. There are also small inflatable pillows and neck-rests that are quick to inflate and will pack up into almost nothing when the air is released. While these are not essential they can be worth taking for a little extra comfort that will mean the difference between a good night's sleep and an uncomfortable night.

## CAMP STOOL OR CHAIR

A stool or chair is a luxury item, but it does allow you to take a rest or eat your meals in comfort off the ground. Consider taking one only if your gear is being carried in a vehicle or on an animal; these are not suitable for lightweight camping trips. Camp stools or chairs are very useful for expeditions that will involve birdwatching or study activities that require you to sit still for lengthy periods of time.

## SITTING MAT

A sitting mat or a piece of foam, about 30 x 60cm/12 x 24in, such as an off-cut from an old sleeping mat, can be used to sit on when you make rest stops, protecting you from damp, wet or uncomfortably rocky ground.

◀ *A neck-rest and eye mask will make your night's sleep or plane journey much more comfortable.*

▼ *A cotton or silk sleeping bag liner will help keep the main sleeping bag clean.*

▲ *A cotton pillowcase stuffed with spare dry clothing will form a perfectly adequate pillow that will increase your comfort at night.*

◀ *Camp stools are made from a very lightweight aluminium and can be folded up for relatively easy packing.*

▲ *Sitting mats are available from outdoor suppliers. They are light enough for day-trippers and backpackers to use.*

▼ *Pack a steel mirror in its waterproof pouch with your wash kit.*

▶ *Board games provide entertainment for relaxation times and can help to promote a good group spirit.*

## BOARD GAMES

These are impractical to carry on lightweight camping trips or where you are unable to accommodate large, bulky items, but otherwise board games can be carried to provide entertainment for evenings and rest days. If only one game is available for a group of people, divide the group into teams or even into a league table to introduce a spirit of competition and encourage team bonding. Pack any counters and dice in a secure bag because if these get lost the game will be unusable.

## STEEL MIRROR

These thin pieces of shiny metal, which can be bought at most camping shops, make shaving and other toilet operations very much easier. If you can, keep the mirror in its own case or plastic envelope, so it will not get wet in your wash kit. The mirror can start to go rusty if it is wet most of the time.

## STOVE WINDSHIELD

A number of stoves have their own small, in-built windshield, but you can buy a larger and more effective one made of cotton or aluminium. This weighs very little but it will make cooking much quicker and more efficient (you are less likely to waste fuel) and can be hugely useful if there is a chance you will need to cook outdoors in high winds.

## ALARM CLOCK

If your wristwatch does not have an alarm setting and you think you will need an alarm call to wake you in the mornings, pack a battery-operated travel alarm clock to be sure you don't sleep right through until lunchtime.

## ADAPTOR

If you travel abroad with electrical equipment that needs to be plugged into a mains socket, you may need to carry an adaptor. Try to find out this kind of information before you travel.

## HANGING SCALES

If you are travelling by plane or with any weight allowance, carrying a set of hanging scales means that you can check you are not exceeding your limit and therefore avoid penalty fines.

## STRETCHERS

These are lengths of reinforced elastic with a hook attached to each end. They can be put to any number of practical uses, from setting up a sheet as a shelter or attaching a mosquito net over your bed to securing a backpack with a broken zip. You can also use them for attaching equipment, such as a sleeping mat, to your pack.

▼ *Three- and two-pin plug adaptors will allow you to use electrical equipment in a mains socket abroad.*

▼ *Carry a good supply of stretchers: they can be rolled up small for easy packing and have a multitude of practical uses.*

▲ *Carry a hanging scale and use it to make sure your luggage is within your weight restriction.*

▲ *If you are a deep sleeper, you may want to carry an alarm clock to be sure you wake in time to make your daily schedule.*

# Tools

Tools are usually heavy and bulky, so most will be restricted to use in a semi-permanent campsite, though some items are available in lightweight versions too. All tools should be kept dry, sharp and in good working condition, and they should always be checked before use for safety's sake.

### SHOVELS
A number of long-handled shovels are essential multi-purpose tools for a base camp. If travelling by vehicle in a desert or wet environment, carry at least one shovel in case you have to dig the vehicle out if you get bogged down. One or two folding entrenching shovels are useful and take up little space. A small plastic trail trowel or shovel, which can weigh only ounces and fits easily into a backpack, will be useful for burying toilet waste.

### MACHETES
These large, heavy-duty chopping knives are very useful if you need to cut a path through thick bush or jungle or clear a campsite of bush and scrub. When buying one make sure it has a good, heavy, sharp blade. You will need a sturdy leather sheath in which to store the machete safely when not in use.

▲ *Axes are dangerous tools in the wrong hands. Make sure they are stored safely.*

▼ *Check your axe is sound before you start to use it.*

▼ *A machete blade has to be kept razor-sharp for the machete to be effective.*

▼ *For safety a machete should be kept in a leather sheath when not in use.*

### AXES
If your kit is to be transported by vehicle and you are going to a remote area you may want to carry a hand axe or a larger felling axe for chopping tree branches to make a camp fire or a temporary shelter.

### SAWS
These are available in a range of sizes, and, for the less experienced, they are easier to use than an axe when cutting up wood. Lightweight campers can carry a small wire saw, which takes up little space and weighs next to nothing.

### REPAIR KITS
Stoves and lighting equipment may need some level of maintenance while you are out in the field. Carry basic tools, such as a screwdriver, that will allow you to make repairs. Some equipment may require a specialized repair kit, so check this when you buy.

▲ *A leather mask on the axe head keeps it clean and protects the blade.*

### DUCT TAPE
This is a strong adhesive tape that can be used to make temporary repairs on almost anything from tents to backpacks to vehicles. Take a large roll of tape, and store it in a lidded container or it will get covered in dust and sand.

◄ *A roll of duct tape is useful for all sorts of running repairs.*

▼ *Check that the saw blade is firmly fixed in the handle before you try to use it.*

▼ *Sharp knives are best carried in a leather sheath for safety. If your knife does not come with its own sheath, try to buy one for it.*

▼ *A Swiss Army penknife is as good as a tool kit, but the blades are small and relatively flimsy and need to be used with care.*

▼ *Folding knives are compact and safer to carry because the blade is protected by the handle.*

## SHARPENING STONES

These are used to keep tools in good working order. All saws, axes, knives and machetes need daily sharpening to remain effective.

▲ *Carry a chain or wire saw in a container and oil it before and after use to keep the saw blade supple.*

▼ *You will need to carry a sharpening stone if you are using axes or saws.*

## PENKNIFE

A penknife, such as a Swiss Army Knife or a Leatherman, is like a pocket-size multi-tool kit. Useful features to look for include straight and serrated blades of various sizes and scissors.

▲ *A multi-purpose Leatherman tool has a host of useful features, including several different blades, saws and scissors.*

### TENT REPAIR KITS

These are available from outdoor suppliers. A typical kit will include several nylon patches, adhesive paste, spare guy ropes and a spare tent peg. Before applying a patch to repair a tear in the tent material clean the area to remove dirt and seal the edges of the patch with adhesive paste to hold it in place.

▼ ▶ *A folding shovel packs neatly away and is useful for digging trenches for camp fires or to dispose of waste.*

# Caring for your Equipment

Camping equipment can be expensive and your safety may depend on it, and it should be looked after if you want it to work properly. Repairs are best done when you return home at the end of a trip, while any faults or damage are still fresh in your mind. Clean, dry and repair the equipment before storing it, so that it is ready for your next trip.

### TENTS

Before packing away your tent after a trip, check that the tent parts are present and in good working order. If the tent is made of a synthetic fabric and the seams are not taped, apply a sealant (available from outdoor equipment suppliers) and allow to dry before the tent is stored. If the tent has a mosquito net on the inside, check the net for holes and get these mended before you use the tent and a mosquito finds them.

### STOVES

A badly maintained stove will not only be inefficient, it can also be dangerous. Never try to use a stove if you think something may be wrong with it. If you need to replace parts, use only genuine manufacturer's parts. Do not store a stove for a long period with fuel in the tank or with a partly used gas cartridge attached to it. Remove the fuel and store separately to the stove.

▼ *Remove the fuel cartridge from a cooking stove before you pack it away and store the two parts separately, preferably in the garage.*

▲ *At the end of your trip check your pack for tears or damage to the zip and seams, and make repairs before you store it away.*

▼ *Wipe your cooking stove clean after every trip, but do this in a well-ventilated place and make sure the stove is switched off first.*

### COMPASSES AND EQUIPMENT WITH ELECTRICAL COMPONENTS

Keep compasses away from magnetic fields, such as an iron or radio speakers. If you have a protractor compass (which is mounted on a clear plastic base) make sure the plastic is kept clean so that the markings can be seen clearly. Batteries should be removed from battery-powered equipment that is not to be used for some time as they can leak and cause corrosion.

### BACKPACKS

When in use, try not to drop or drag a loaded backpack, and do not carry it by only one strap. When you return home after a trip, empty the pack and wipe it clean inside and out with a damp cloth and check the seams for tears and holes. Make sure it is dry

▲ *Backpacks should be wiped with a damp cloth after use. Allow the pack to dry out and then store it in a well-ventilated place.*

▼ *The plastic base of a protractor compass needs to be wiped clean after use to keep the base free of dirt and the markings readable.*

before storing away. If your pack is very dirty, wash it in soap flakes and water but do not use detergents as they can destroy the waterproofing properties of the fabric. Packs should be stored in a dry, well-ventilated place.

### SLEEPING BAGS

With the exception of fibre-pile bags, all sleeping bags need to be cleaned carefully and they all take a long time to dry out thoroughly. If you have your bag dry-cleaned, air it for at least half a day before you use it to get rid of the fumes from the chemicals. If you wash your bag in a washing machine dry it flat as line-drying can damage the bag's construction. If you use a bag liner, be it silk or cotton, this should be cleaned according to the manufacturer's instructions at the end of every trip.

### Feather or down filling

It is safest to take a feather-filled bag to a dry-cleaners and ask them to clean it in the same way as they would a feather or down duvet. If you prefer to wash it, use a specialist product designed for the job, then dry the bag flat. While the bag is drying, break up the clumps of down. When almost dry, shake the bag to distribute the filling. When dry, store it by hanging it in a warm, dry place.

### Synthetic filling

A synthetic bag should be hand-washed without detergents and dried slowly in a well-ventilated place or in a tumble drier on a low heat. Synthetic bags can also be dry-cleaned.

### Fibre-pile filling

These are the easiest bags to clean. Just put them in your washing machine, using a soap-based powder rather than a detergent, and line-dry. Fibre-pile bags will dry very quickly.

### FOOTWEAR

As expensive and important pieces of kit, footwear needs special care during your trip and when you return home.

### During your trip

When you take off your boots at the end of each day, shake them and tap firmly together to get rid of loose dirt. Prise mud out from the treads with a penknife. Allow the boots to dry out as best you can: stuff the insides with scrunched up newspaper and leave overnight in the door of your tent or hang them outside if it isn't raining. Do not dry boots in front of a camp fire or in the hot sun because this can ruin the uppers.

### At the end of the trip

Remove all traces of dirt and mud, then wash the boots in warm soapy water and allow them to dry naturally. All footwear needs to be reproofed in order to waterproof the uppers before

▲ *To dry wet walking boots, stuff the insides with sheets of newspaper or long grass and leave overnight in a dry place.*

further use; leather that isn't regularly treated with a wax or oil-based product will eventually dry out and crack. If your walking boots or shoes are made of leather give them two coats of polish, wax dubbin, oil or a recommended product before storage. If your boots are made of fabric use a recommended silicone-based product, which can be either sprayed or rubbed on.

## CARING FOR WALKING BOOTS

**1** With a boot on the end of each hand tap your boots together to knock off any loose pieces of mud and dirt.

**2** Using a penknife or small stick, prise mud and dirt from between the treads on the underside of each boot.

**3** Using a hard-bristled brush, firmly brush each boot all over to remove any remaining mud, dirt and dust.

**4** Check that the laces on each boot are not frayed and replace if necessary. Wash the boots in warm soapy water.

**5** Use your fingers or a soft cloth to apply an oil-based waterproofing product to leather boots or shoes.

**6** Protect fabric walking boots with a silicone-based waterproofing product recommended by the manufacturer.

# Preparing your Equipment

Before setting off on any trip in the outdoors, whether it is a day's walking in your local area or a month-long expedition to another country, you should check the equipment you are taking with you. Any items showing signs of wear will need to be repaired or replaced. It is far easier to carry out major repairs at home, where materials and replacements are available, rather than out in the field.

### CLOTHING AND FOOTWEAR

As well as making sure your outdoor clothing is suitable for the climate and planned activities, you need to check that key items such as shirts and trousers still fit you comfortably, especially if you have not worn them for a while – you may have put on or lost weight since your last trip. Check the condition of your clothing and repair as necessary, paying particular attention to zips and buttons as these

▲ *Protective sealants can be applied to the seams of clothing to strengthen the stitches and maintain the waterproofing qualities.*

are likely candidates to break or fall off under the pressure of use. If you are travelling in a group with a number of other people, you may want to mark personal kit and clothing with your name or an identifying mark.

Check that your walking boots are clean and in good working order. Stitching on the seams needs to be intact; if it isn't you could take the boots to a shoe repair shop or sew the stitching yourself using a bradawl or awl and a strong needle. Intact seams should be coated with a sealant to protect the stitches.

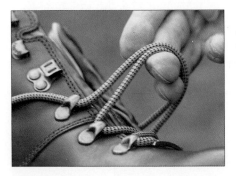

◄ *Ordinary boot polish can be used on leather boots but fabric boots will need a recommended silicone-based product.*

▲ *Always check the head and shaft of your axe. A head that comes loose when in use can result in a nasty, if not fatal, accident.*

Small splits in the leather or fabric uppers of boots can be repaired at home with an adhesive. A shoe repair shop may be able to patch up large tears, otherwise you will need to replace the boots: large tears will let in water or sand and dirt and they will worsen with use during the trip. Replace frayed laces and take at least one spare pair of laces with you.

Check that the sole is not coming away from the main boot; if it is you may be able to get it repaired at a shoe repair shop or you may need new boots. Reproof or polish leather boots before every trip (and again when you return home) to maintain the condition of the leather, and treat fabric walking boots with a silicone-based product.

### CHECKING YOUR BOOTS

**1** Check boot laces for damage or early signs of fraying that may cause them to break under the pressure of hard use. Fit new laces if needed and carry spares.

**2** Check that none of the D-rings is bent or broken and make sure they are free of mud or dirt from previous trips, which may make it difficult to fit laces.

**3** Look closely at the stitching all the way round each boot, and organize repairs for any that is loose. Apply a sealant to waterproof the stitches.

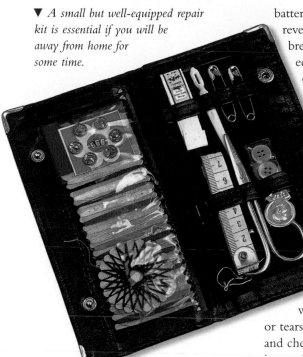

▼ *A small but well-equipped repair kit is essential if you will be away from home for some time.*

battery, once you have checked it, reverse one of the batteries so as to break the circuit, which means the equipment cannot be switched on by mistake. Carry correctly sized spare batteries for all your equipment, including lithium batteries for camera or computer equipment.

## CAMPING EQUIPMENT

Check that your tent has all its parts and enough pegs to put it up as well as some spare, and that everything is in working order. Look for holes or tears in the tent and groundsheet, and check that the guying points are in good condition. Check that your sleeping bag is clean and that the zip, if there is one, works properly.

## COOKING EQUIPMENT

Try out your stove to make sure it is working and check you have sufficient fuel to last the duration of your trip unless you know for certain that you will be able to buy that particular type of fuel at your destination. If you are travelling by plane you will not be able to carry fuel with you, so part-used gas containers should be removed from your stove. Crockery and utensils should be clean and supplies of washing-up liquid and condiments replenished. Check that pan handles are not damaged, that pan lids fit properly, and that your water containers do not leak.

## BATTERY-POWERED EQUIPMENT

Equipment that requires batteries should have had them removed when they were last used, as leaking batteries can cause corrosion. If this wasn't done and a battery has leaked, you may be able to remove any corrosion with an emery file or a piece of abrasive paper. (It will be a lot easier to do this now at home than in some cold field at dusk when your torch does not work.) Check all of the battery terminals for corrosion, and remove any that you find. If this is not successful the item may need to be replaced. Otherwise, put new batteries into the equipment and check that it works properly. If equipment requires more than one

▲ *Gas stoves are awkward shapes but they can be packed into pouch bags designed for the purpose for easy storage and transit.*

▼ *Check that you have enough fuel for the trip. If you haven't used your stove for a while try it out to make sure it works.*

## CARRYING EQUIPMENT

Your backpack should be clean, with all straps and/or zips undamaged. Repair any straps that appear to be loose or weak, paying attention to the waist belt and shoulder straps of large backpacks, which take the bulk of the weight. Apply a sealant to waterproof all of the seams.

▶ *Always make sure your first-aid kit has been properly restocked before setting out on a trip.*

▼ *Check the straps on your pack and make any repairs while you are still at home. Weak straps can break easily under pressure.*

▼ *Make sure the zips and seams on your pack are intact and apply a protective sealant to the seams to reinforce the stitches.*

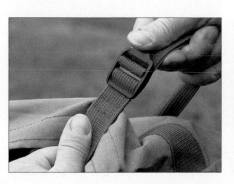

# ORIENTEERING & CAMPCRAFT

While camping you are at the mercy of natural forces, and your activities will be dominated by the times of sunrise and sunset, changes in the weather, the lie of the land, the nearest water and the supply of fuel.

Your comfort will depend on your skills in choosing a suitable site, erecting a shelter, building a fire and establishing a smooth routine.

When you leave there should be no trace of your stay.

# Navigation by the Sun, Moon and Stars

Modern man has so many distractions and gadgets that we often fail to notice all the help that nature can give us in finding our way around. There is no doubt that navigating by map and compass is efficient and accurate, but what happens if you are deprived of these tools, if you lose your map or damage your compass?

The heavenly bodies behave in predictable ways, predictions that were worked out by our ancient ancestors and have been used for navigation for centuries. In the event of lost or damaged equipment your ability to use the sun, the moon and the stars to monitor your direction could be a lifesaver, and it pays to commit a few basic principles to memory.

Practise each of the following natural navigation methods before you travel and afterwards use your map and compass to check how you did. Not only will it give you faith in the accuracy of natural signposts, it will also boost your confidence in your own abilities as a navigator. Seasoned navigators are aware of and actively read the signs provided by nature at all times, no matter how sophisticated their modern equipment. After all, the ability to navigate accurately is the most important bushcraft skill of all.

## USING THE SUN

The sun rises in the east and sets in the west every day wherever you are in the world, so you may want to take note of obvious geographical features that are in line with the sunrise or sunset to give you a rough sense of direction for use throughout the day. The techniques outlined below are only useful if the sun is visible, but even with a heavy cloud cover it is usually possible to detect the lightening of the sky that happens at sunrise. This can then be noted for use later in the day.

In the northern hemisphere the sun will be due south at noon and in the southern hemisphere it will be due north. The techniques below are at their most accurate when carried out as near to local noon as possible.

### INACCURATE READINGS

The nearer you are to the equator the less accurate any attempt to find a direction using the sun will be. When the sun is almost directly overhead it is extremely difficult to determine its direction.

## Finding north and south using your wristwatch

To do this you will need a traditional analogue watch with two hands set at local time (without variation for summer daylight savings, which do not match real time) and held horizontally. If you are in the northern hemisphere, point the hour hand of your watch towards the sun. Imagine a line halfway between the hour hand and the 12. This line will be pointing roughly south. If you are in the southern hemisphere, point the 12 at the sun and an imaginary line between the 12 and the hour hand will give you a rough indication of north.

## FINDING NORTH AND SOUTH USING A WRISTWATCH

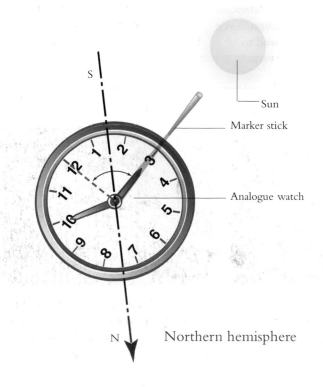

S

Sun

Marker stick

Analogue watch

N    Northern hemisphere

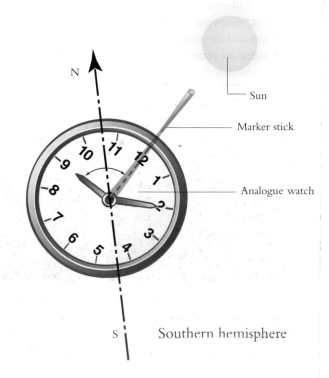

N

Sun

Marker stick

Analogue watch

S    Southern hemisphere

### SEASONAL VARIATION

It is a well-known fact that the sun rises in the east and sets in the west, but what is less well known is that the sun does not rise and set *exactly* in the east and west. There is some seasonal variation, and you may need to bear this in mind if you need to make decisions based on the general rule.

## Finding east and west using the shadow stick method

This is a useful method if you are in open country and can afford the time to stop for a while. It works at any time of the day when there is sunshine of any strength, and at any latitude or in either hemisphere.

Select a stick about 90–120cm/3–4ft long and as upright as possible. Plant the stick into a piece of flat ground that is not overlooked by trees, vegetation or any other geological formations. Mark where the tip of the shadow falls with a pebble. Wait for 15–20 minutes and mark where the tip of the new shadow falls, then join the two points together. This line will run east–west with the first point marked being west.

If you will be in your location from the early morning and have time to wait there for almost the entire day, you can try an alternative method using a shadow stick, and the reward is that this is usually more accurate. Plant a stick about 90–120cm/3–4ft long and as upright as possible into the flat, open ground and mark the first shadow tip in the morning. Draw a smooth arc in the ground at exactly this distance from the stick, using the stick as the centre point of the arc. As noon approaches, the shadow will shrink. During the afternoon, the shadow will start to lengthen again, and you need to mark the exact point where it touches the arc. Join up the two points to give an east–west reference, with the mark made in the morning being west.

▲ *Try to be aware of the general direction of the sunrise and sunset at all times, even when you do not need to orienteer yourself.*

### WHAT'S IN A SHADOW?

The way a shadow moves can indicate which hemisphere you are in: clockwise in the northern hemisphere and anticlockwise in the southern hemisphere. A shadow can also be used as a guide to both direction and the time of day.

## SHADOW STICK METHOD

**1** Plant a stick of 90–120cm/3–4ft and as straight as possible into a flat, open piece of ground. Mark the tip of the shadow that forms with a pebble.

**2** Wait for about 15–20 minutes before checking the shadow. It will now have moved, so mark the tip of the new shadow with another pebble.

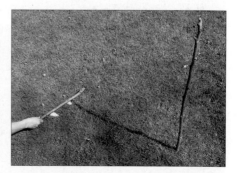

**3** Lay a stick on the ground to connect the two pebbles. The line that it forms will give you an east–west reference, with the first pebble being west.

▶ *A moon that is not hidden behind clouds may be able to direct you to reference points for north–south and east–west.*

## USING THE MOON

Unlike the sun the moon has a highly variable pattern of visibility and it is far less bright than the sun. As a result its usefulness as a navigational aid is much more limited, particularly in cloudy conditions when the moon can be almost completely obscured.

The moon reflects the light of the sun and as the moon travels around the earth we see different amounts of its sunlit face, ranging from a sliver crescent through to a full moon. When the moon lies between the sun and the earth the side of the moon facing the earth has no sunlight so we cannot see it at all: this is called a new moon. It takes 29.5 days for the moon to travel round the earth.

If the moon rises before the sun has completely set, the visible side of the moon (which is the side illuminated by the sun) will be on the west. If the moon rises after midnight, when there is no sun, the visible side of the moon will be on the east. A basic rule to remember for an east–west reference at night is that if you can see the moon rising you are facing east, and if you can see it setting you are facing west. This will apply whichever hemisphere you are in.

### Finding north and south using a crescent moon

If the moon is not full, and is not obscured by cloud, you will be able to work out a simple north or south reference during the night. Looking up at the moon, imagine a line drawn through the two tips of the crescent moon and continue the line all the way down to the horizon. If the two tips of the crescent are on the left, the point where the imaginary line meets the horizon will be roughly south in the northern hemisphere and roughly north in the southern hemisphere. If the tips of the crescent are on the right the reverse is true, and the point at which the imaginary line meets the horizon will indicate north in the northern hemisphere and south in the southern hemisphere.

▼ *The diagram below shows how to find north or south using a crescent moon. The dotted line connects the tips of the left-hand moon and meets the horizon at a point that is south in the northern hemisphere and north in the southern hemisphere. The right-hand moon shows the other way a crescent moon can appear. Here, the dotted line intersects the horizon at north in the northern hemisphere and south in the southern hemisphere.*

▲ *The North Star lies above the North Pole and can be found by running a line into the sky from the far side of the Plough's pan.*

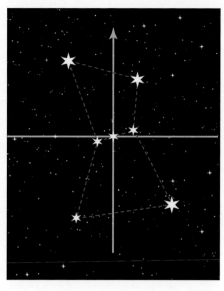

▲ *An imaginary line drawn across the middle of the Orion constellation lies roughly east–west in the northern hemisphere.*

▲ *The Southern Cross will help you to find south in the southern hemisphere. Note the false cross of dimmer stars to the right.*

## USING THE STARS

Because of the many and varied constellations, navigation by the stars is by far the most complex part of celestial navigation and therefore the most difficult to commit to memory. The constellations and individual stars visible from the two hemispheres differ, and this adds to the difficulty. Despite this, stars have been used for navigation for tens of thousands of years.

As the earth is constantly moving, note that the star constellations may appear upside down or sideways when compared to the above diagrams. Like the sun, star constellations always rise in the east and set in the west.

### In the northern hemisphere

To find north, locate the North Star or Polaris, which lies over the North Pole. This is one of the brightest stars in the sky and the only one that appears to remain static. To locate it, first find the pan-shaped constellation known as the Plough or Big Dipper. Follow the two stars that form the far side of the pan for six times the distance between them; this will bring you to the North Star.

To find an east–west line, use the star constellation known as Orion or the Hunter. A line taken through the three stars that make up the Hunter's belt lies roughly east–west.

### In the southern hemisphere

The North Star is not visible in the southern hemisphere and there is no equivalent star coveniently lying over the South Pole. Instead you can use the Southern Cross constellation. To find it, look towards the middle of the Milky Way where there is a dark area known as the Coal Sack. Straddling this area is the Southern Cross: four bright stars forming a cross plus a fifth fainter star and two bright pointer stars. (A false cross of dimmer stars lies to the right.) Follow the longest line through the cross and down four-and-a-half times its length, then look down to the horizon and that will be due south.

### NAVIGATIONAL STARS

**North Star** Also known as Polaris and the Pole Star. Located above the North Pole it is a key reference for north. It is the only star that remains static; all other stars move around it.
**The Plough** Also known as the Big Dipper. It forms part of the large Great Bear star constellation.
**Orion** Also known as the Hunter. This rises above the Equator and can be seen in both hemispheres.
**Milky Way** A hazy band of millions of stars that stretches across the sky. In the middle of it is the Coal Sack.

### MARKING YOUR DIRECTION

When using the moon and stars as navigational tools, do not forget that they will not be visible the next day when the sun has risen. If you are not planning to start on your course straight away during the night, you will need to mark the direction to give yourself a reference point for the morning. Mark your course with a stick or identify it with a prominent object on the horizon, so that you will know which way to go without your guiding moon and stars.

▲ *Remember to mark the direction with a stick or a pebble before daylight breaks.*

# Choosing a Campsite

There are very few perfect campsites, so when choosing a site you will probably have to compromise to some extent. Obviously your priorities will vary depending on how long you are going to stay there, and how large your camp will be, but it is a good idea to have some general principles in mind during the selection process so that you know what to look out for.

### RECONNAISSANCE

For a long-term campsite, particularly for a large group, you will need to plan ahead and may have already visited the site before the group arrives. If you choose a site on private land you will need the landowner's permission to camp. However, whether you are looking at an established site or scouting in the wilderness, the points to check are the same.

### WHEN TO LOOK

If your campsite is to be an overnight stop on the trail you should start to look for a suitable place at least two to three hours before it gets dark. By that time you will need to have settled in and pitched your tents and your food preparations should be well under way. Be prepared to stop short of your intended destination for that day if you find a spot that looks ideal. You may even want to backtrack a little if you do go on but the terrain ahead fails to offer further viable sites.

### WHAT TO LOOK FOR

Try to avoid extreme conditions of any kind. In hot countries you will find it a great advantage to have some natural shade on your campsite. In colder areas your priority is likely to be natural shelter from wind. Always try to find a site that is well drained; this usually means looking for a reasonably high site. Not only will you avoid marshy, damp ground, but you will also not

▶ *Make sure you set up your camp well above the high-tide mark if you are camping near tidal water.*

▲ *In hot countries shade on your campsite will be a great advantage. If you want to use a popular site you will need to book ahead.*

find yourself in a pocket of cold air during the night. If it is windy, you will need space to pitch your tents with the doors facing away from the wind.

It will be an advantage if the site has its own water supply but you should always check to see where the water

comes from. Just because local people drink it, it does not mean it is safe for you to drink. Unless you have good evidence to the contrary, you should always regard water as contaminated and treat it accordingly. Don't be tempted to camp too near a water

▼ *Camping by a river can be noisy. Make sure that, if it floods, your camp is high enough above the river not to be affected.*

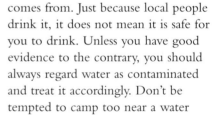

**CAMPSITE CHECKLIST**

Check to see if the site is protected from the prevailing wind and that there is a readily available water supply. Once these criteria are satisfied, assess the following points, depending on your area and situation:

- The ground is reasonably level and flat, and is not covered with sharp stones or pieces of wood that could damage your groundsheet or sleeping mat.
- The land is not in a hollow, where a pocket of cold air could collect during the night.
- The land is not in a dried-up watercourse, which could flood without warning.
- The ground is neither boggy nor likely to become boggy.
- You have checked to see if you need permission to camp and have agreed any fees to be paid.

- You are happy that you can drive your tent pegs into the ground or that you can anchor the guy lines in some other way.
- There are no branches or unsafe trees near your tent site or dry-stone walls or other loose stones that are near enough to collapse on your tent or you while you are asleep.
- If the site is near to water, it is well above the flood level of a river or the high-tide mark at the coast, and there is no danger of crocodiles.
- There are no insect nests nearby and no holes or bushes where snakes may live.
- In a hot climate, there is adequate shade from the sun.
- You are not too near a source of water or a patch of wetland that will attract insects and animals during the night.

- There is a plentiful supply of wood for your fire. Unless you have permission, you should use only dead wood or wood lying on the ground.
- The camping area has not previously been used by domestic animals or livestock, which could have left ticks and other insects on the ground.
- There are no domestic animals or livestock in the field and no obvious signs of game trails going through the camp.
- In the mountains, your campsite is protected from a snow avalanche or rock falls from above.
- If the ground is covered in snow, you have stuck a ski pole or stripped tree branch into the snow to see if the ground is firm all over your site, with no hidden crevasses.

source, such as a stream, as it may attract clouds of biting insects in the evening, and may be a place where animals come to drink.

In an area where there is the possibility of attack by bandits or a track record of theft from tourists, it

can be worth calling at a local police post and asking them for advice on where you can camp safely. They will sometimes offer you a site in their own compound. If you are camping in a place – or travelling through the area – for any length of time, try to

build and maintain good relationships with the local people, especially the community leaders. You may find that during your stay you need their help obtaining supplies or settling disputes between yourselves and other local people or traders.

▼ *Trees with seriously undermined roots might be felled by a high wind, so it could be risky to camp near them.*

▼ *If you have to camp among trees check that there are no rotten or broken branches above the area where you pitch your tent.*

▼ *Get some local knowledge about the site: a watercourse may be subject to flooding in the event of heavy rain many miles away.*

# Camp Layout

The layout of your camp will be dictated by the site you have chosen, the climatic conditions, the size of the camp and personal preferences. There are, however, some golden rules that should be followed for the sake of the safety and well-being of the campers.

## POSITIONING TENTS

Try to pitch the tents with their back into the prevailing wind. If possible, use either a belt of trees or bushes to form a natural windbreak. If hot weather conditions make shade important then choose a place under some trees, but remember that falling twigs and branches will be likely. Make sure your sleeping area is well away from the cooking area and toilet area, and upwind of them if there is a prevailing wind.

## TOILETS

If there are no permanent toilets on the site, construct a toilet area downwind of the tents and away from sleeping and cooking areas, with natural screening or a bivvy bag or groundsheet for privacy. You can dig a hole in the ground with a trowel or knife for solid waste, covering it with soil after use and burning toilet paper. Have a separate urination point. Alternatively, you can dig a large ditch to make a latrine, covering it with soil each time it is used. Note that latrines can become a breeding ground for germs unless the soil covering is applied religiously after every use.

### USING WATER WISELY

If your camp is near a stream or river use the water systematically:
- Collect water for drinking and cooking upstream of the site. Make sure you are also upstream of animals' drinking spots.
- Wash yourself midstream.
- Wash dishes downstream, scraping food remnants off before rinsing. You can wash clothes downstream but do not use detergent as it will pollute the water.

▲ *A campsite under trees has the advantage of being shady, but you risk twigs and branches falling on your tent.*

## WASHING AREA

If you are going to have an area dedicated to washing clothes, keep this away from the cooking and sleeping areas. Site any clothes lines well away from where people will be walking, especially at night.

## WHERE TO SITE A FIRE

If you are going to have a fire, light it well away from the tents, as sparks can fly out and burn holes in the material. Also make sure it is downwind of the tents, on a flat area well away from trees and bushes.

## KITCHEN

Site the food preparation area some distance from where you will be sleeping, so that if an animal is attracted by the smells of food during the night, you will not be disturbed. Also, any flies attracted to your cooking will be well away from your sleeping area. If you can, have an extra tent near the cooking area for the storage of food. Do not keep food inside a tent where anyone is sleeping.

## SOCIAL CENTRE

Choose an area away from the sleeping and cooking areas where you can set up a working and/or social area in which people can sit and talk or work. This area will become the social centre of the camp. Make sure that everyone accepts responsibility for keeping this shared area clean and tidy.

## PARKING AREA

A large campsite will probably be accessible by road or track. If your group is travelling by vehicle, allocate a parking area and make it clear that vehicles cannot drive around within the camp itself, which could be dangerous.

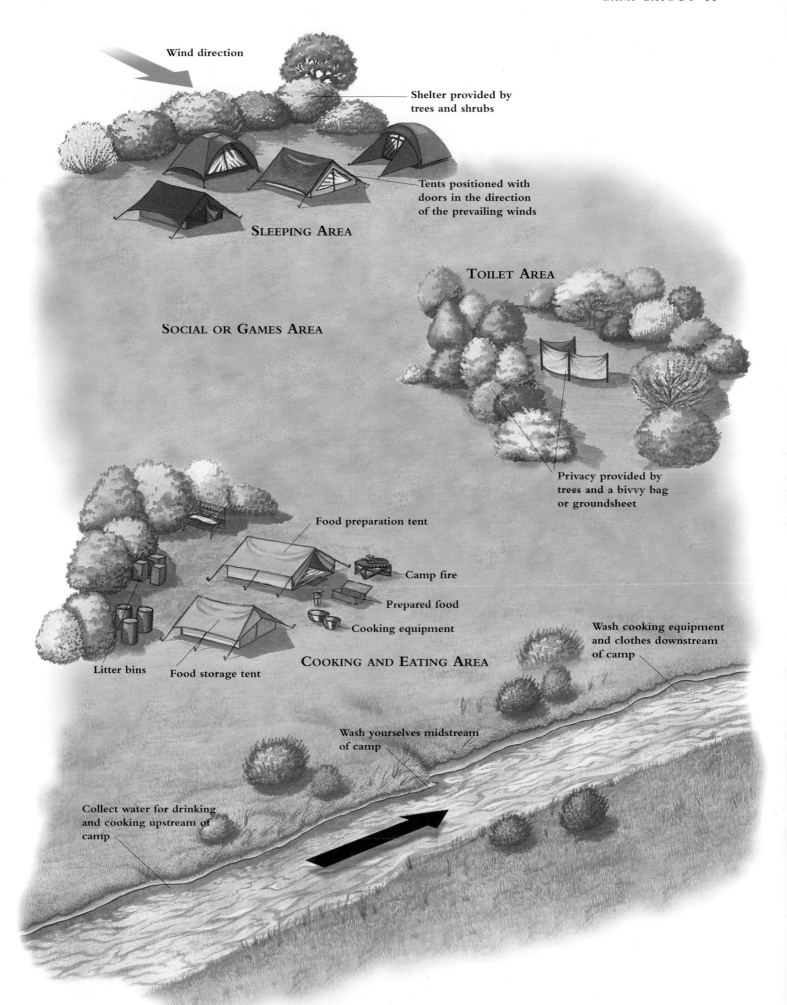

Wind direction

Shelter provided by trees and shrubs

Tents positioned with doors in the direction of the prevailing winds

**SLEEPING AREA**

**TOILET AREA**

**SOCIAL OR GAMES AREA**

Privacy provided by trees and a bivvy bag or groundsheet

Food preparation tent

Camp fire

Prepared food

Cooking equipment

Wash cooking equipment and clothes downstream of camp

Litter bins

Food storage tent

**COOKING AND EATING AREA**

Wash yourselves midstream of camp

Collect water for drinking and cooking upstream of camp

# Erecting Tents

Once you have checked your site for suitability you can get on with erecting your tent. No matter what kind of tent it is, you will need to follow the same system of erection. You should refer to the manufacturer's instructions, especially if this is the first time you have put the tent up, but your memory may also need refreshing if there has been a long gap since you last did it.

It's a wise precaution to practise erecting and striking your tent before you go away (you can do this in the garden or a local open space), so that you iron out any problems and can do the job quickly. On the expedition

▶ *The geodesic dome (shown here without the outer tent) is very strong, but if any of the poles break it will lose its strength.*

## ERECTING A DOME TENT

**1** Check that you have all of the tent parts. If the inner tent needs to be attached to the outer tent, do it now. Make sure that all zips are closed.

**2** Assemble the poles and thread them through the sleeves in the tent. It is easier to push them: pulling them may pull the pole sections apart.

**3** Now place the ends of the poles in the fastenings provided in the lower part of the tent so that they put the whole of the tent under tension.

**4** Peg out the inner tent. Always push the pegs in at an angle away from the tent. This prevents the pegs from being easily pulled up by the wind.

**5** Peg out the outer tent and check to see that the inner tent is attached correctly. If you need to reposition a peg, use another peg to pull it out.

**6** Peg out all the remaining guy lines. Gather up any remaining pegs, place them in the tent bag and stow the bag inside the tent.

there may be days when weather conditions are bad and you are forced to pitch your tent in windy or rainy weather, or even in the dark, so the more familiar you can become with the procedure in advance, the better. If you erect the tent using the same procedure each time it will become automatic.

If you are using a tent made of cotton, it is better to pitch it and get it thoroughly wet, then let it dry out naturally before using it.

**CHECKING THE SITE**
The first thing to do is to check the piece of ground on which you intend putting the tent. Make sure it is flat and does not dip in a way that will mean water collects there if it rains. Is the

ground soft enough for you to drive the tent pegs into it? Is it reasonably sheltered from the wind but not too near anything that might crash down on to it, such as a dead tree? When you are happy with the lie of the land, the

next thing is to make sure that there are no sharp objects that could damage the groundsheet, such as stones and twigs. Clear anything of this kind from the site and if necessary remove or flatten any small humps.

▶ *The traditional ridge tent is still widely used on expeditions. It is simple to erect and will withstand a lot of bad weather.*

## ERECTING A RIDGE TENT

**1** Take the tent out of the bag and check to make sure all the parts are present, then lay out the inner tent on the ground and peg down the corners.

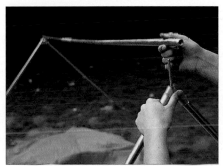

**2** Assemble the frame over the inner tent. Check the poles before fitting them together as incorrect connections can be hard to unfasten.

**3** Attach the inner tent to the poles using the fittings provided. Place the flysheet over the poles and where necessary attach to the inner tent.

**4** Peg out the guy lines on the flysheet, starting with the four corners. Make sure all the door zips are closed while you do this.

**5** Complete the pegging out of all pegging points and guy lines. The flysheet should be tightly stretched and should not be touching the inner tent.

**6** Undo the door zip for ventilation and tie at the sides to secure. Adjust the guy lines so that the walls of the flysheet are clear of the inner tent.

## ASSEMBLING THE PARTS

If it is a new tent, read the instructions and check that you have all the parts. With most tents, you will put the inner tent up first, but do check the instructions about this. First assemble the poles and get the pegs out of their bag. Then, depending on the type of tent, start your pitching routine. Make sure all the doors are closed when pitching the tent. If you cannot erect your tent on your own, make sure other people are available to help.

Many modern tents, especially geodesic domes, have quite thin poles. To strengthen them, wrap tape around each pole where it fits into the next joint. This will stop the joints splitting in high winds.

▶ *The weather may be calm when you put your tent up, but always use all guy lines provided in case it changes for the worse.*

## ERECTING A FAMILY TENT

**1** Take the tent out of its bag and check with the instructions that you have all the parts – the pegs, inner and outer tents, poles and guy lines.

**2** Lift the poles forming the main assembly to pull the tent up into position.

**3** Lock the joints in the poles to create the tent frame.

**4** Slide any additional poles into their sleeves. Assemble the porch area, taking care not to damage either the tent fabric or the poles.

**5** Peg out the sides of the tent, sticking the tent pegs firmly into the ground and angling them to pull the guy lines away from the tent.

**6** If your tent has a separate inner it may be necessary to attach it at this stage, then peg it out. Add the flysheet and peg out all of the guy lines.

## ERECTING A PATROL TENT

**1** Take the tent out of its bag and check that you have all the parts.

**2** Spread the main tent out, upside down, on the ground.

**3** Place the ridge pole in the sleeve or loops provided in the main tent.

**4** Push the spikes on the two uprights into each end of the ridge pole.

**5** Push the spikes through the reinforced holes in the tent canvas.

**6** Pull the canvas back over the poles and attach the main guylines.

**7** With someone at each end holding one of the poles firmly, lift the tent into an upright position.

**8** Peg out the main guy lines so that the frame of the tent will stand up on its own.

**9** Now make sure the door flaps are closed, either by lacing them together or by closing the zip.

**10** Peg out the walls. Check they will be under the roof so that rain will clear them when it runs off the roof.

**11** Peg out the side guy lines of the tent to create the walls.

**12** Check the whole tent. If it does not have a sewn-in groundsheet, lay out the groundsheet inside the tent.

# Base Camps

For a long or large-scale expedition exploring challenging and inaccessible terrain or requiring a large amount of equipment, it is usually necessary to set up an initial camp to act as a semi-permanent support structure. From this "home base" more lightly equipped expeditions can set off, for instance to trek through wilderness, climb a mountain or conduct an archaeological survey. The base camp acts as a communications hub and supply store. It is likely to be sited in an area that is accessible by motor vehicles and can generally offer a reasonably high degree of comfort.

Setting up this more elaborate kind of camp is naturally a much more complex operation than setting up a small temporary camp. You will probably be using heavier and bigger tents, your cooking area will be of a more permanent nature and you will need to construct a toilet area and make provision for rubbish disposal.

## CAMP ROUTINE

You will find it useful to draw up a simple and sensible set of rules that everyone is able to follow. If there are a lot of people in the camp, you may want to post up a programme each day listing meal times and any planned events or meetings. It is also a good idea to have either a lights-out time or a quiet time, so that those who want to sleep can; you should also try to implement this rule if your camp is set up near other people, who will not want to be kept awake.

## CAMP SECURITY

If you are a large party with people coming and going, perhaps sometimes overnight, make sure you have a system of knowing who is where and who will be in camp when. This will not only act as a general safety feature, letting you know where all the members of the group are at any one time, but will also aid with planning the catering.

▲ *A base camp may need to include many different components. Draw up a logical plan for its layout before pitching any tents.*

If there will be times when all or most of the members of the expedition are going to be away from the camp it is a good idea to employ a local person to act as a guard. Even when the camp is not empty, your equipment should not be left lying around in case it is stolen or damaged.

▼ *Long-stay camps need to be supplied with well-maintained and carefully sited toilet and washing facilities.*

### BURNING WASTE

Not all waste will be suitable for burning on the camp fire, and a large long-term campsite may require an incinerator, which should be carefully sited well away from the tents. This could be an ordinary galvanized incinerator of the kind intended for garden waste, or you could make one by piercing holes all around an oil drum or metal bin and siting it over an open fire. The ashes should be removed regularly and buried in a pit used for solid waste.

▲ *A daily discussion and briefing involving all the group members will help to keep the base camp running smoothly.*

▲ *A large camp will probably require one or two designated cooks to provide regular meals for the whole party.*

## KITCHEN

Hygiene should be a priority in the food preparation area in a large camp. Make sure your kitchen area is kept thoroughly clean and that all waste is properly disposed of each day so it will not attract animals and insects. With a lot of people living together, poor hygiene can quickly result in everyone getting ill, especially in hot countries.

Wash all the cooking pots and equipment in hot water each day. Try to have some hot water on your fire or stove all the time so that people arriving back from activities can always have a hot drink or even some hot water to wash in.

If possible, rig up some sort of structure that enables you to store your eating and cooking equipment, and all your food, off the ground. This is useful and more hygienic than leaving them on the ground. Some kind of table or raised surface also makes the preparation of food much easier if you are cooking for a large group. All fresh food should be stored in sealed containers or cool boxes.

If you are using a fire to cook on, make sure your woodpile is kept tidy and well stocked. Your reserves of water should always be kept covered and should be well marked to show which water is for drinking and which is for washing.

## BURYING WASTE

In a camp that will be occupied for some time it is particularly important not to leave any waste lying around. Waste food will encourage wild animals to scavenge in the camp and will attract flies. If you are allowed to do so on your site, dig two pits at least 60cm/2ft deep: in one you should dispose of any solid waste, such as flattened cans; the other is for the disposal of any cooking or waste water.

Each time you put anything into the first pit, cover it with soil to prevent insects from feeding on the waste. Make sure this pit is well marked so that nobody steps in it. If you are going to bury cans or other packaging, burn and flatten them first.

Place a layer of bracken or grass over the top of the second pit to filter out any scraps of food that may be in the cooking water. This covering should be burnt or buried every day.

### CAMP LAYOUT

A large base camp may need to accommodate the following specific areas, whose siting needs to be planned before you start pitching the tents:

- Camp fire: should be central but downwind of the tents.
- Woodpile: near the fire. The wood, especially the kindling, will need a cover to keep it dry.
- Chopping area: next to the woodpile, and clearly marked out to avoid accidents.
- Kitchen area: should be sheltered, fairly near the camp fire and away from the tents, and ideally near the water supply.
- First aid tent: in a large base camp everyone should know where to find the first-aid kit in an emergency situation.
- Storage: should be conveniently sited depending on its use. If you do not have a dedicated first aid tent, keep the first-aid kit near the door of a storage tent.
- Toilets: should be downwind of the site and screened off, but not so far away from the tents that people are tempted to use a nearby bush instead.

# Lightweight Camping

This form of camping is so-called because the weight of your camping gear is cut to a minimum, allowing you to transport it under your own steam. All the equipment you use will have been selected because it is made of lightweight material and made to be either carried in a backpack or packed into a canoe or cycle pannier bags.

### MINIMIZING YOUR LOAD
Lightweight camping can be an end in itself, although most people use it as a means of carrying out some other kind of activity, such as walking, cycling or paddling in the countryside. The real enthusiasts believe that you should be able to go away for, say, a weekend's expedition on your own taking kit weighing no more than 9kg/20lb. Getting your load down to this level requires practice and experience. However, if you are travelling with another person the target is much

▼ *Lightweight camping gives you the freedom to explore inaccessible areas that few others will be able to reach.*

easier to reach, as much of what you take, including your tent, stove, fuel and cooking equipment, will be shared between you.

### CHOOSING EQUIPMENT
If it is to combine the high performance you need when camping with extremely lightweight and compact design, all your equipment needs to be of the best quality. This means it will not come cheap, and you may well find that you have to carry more weight to begin with and acquire better, lighter pieces of kit over time. Very lightweight equipment tends also to be more susceptible to damage; you will need to treat it with care and maintain it well, following the manufacturers' instructions.

Much of the art of travelling light lies in the care with which you choose what to take. Thinking very carefully about where you are going and the kind of terrain you will be travelling over will help you to avoid carrying unnecessary items. The more trips you do, the better you will know how

Overloading a cycle, kayak or canoe can make it dangerously unstable, and, if you are walking, carrying too heavy a load will be wearisome and spoil your trip.

Your equipment should weigh no more than 11kg/25lb and, with some care, you should be able to get it down to 9kg/20lb.

When you have all your equipment together, consider how you could reduce its weight.
- Is everything you have essential?
- Do you need to carry the containers some of the equipment may be packed in?
- Do you need all the things in your washing kit? Could you cut the soap in half and take a smaller tube of toothpaste?
- Do you need a knife, fork and spoon, or could you get by with just a spoon?
- Do you really need all the clothes you are thinking of taking?

much is really essential. After every lightweight camping trip, put all your gear into three piles: "used a lot", "used sometimes" and "never used". Retain any items from the last pile that are your safety equipment, then get rid of the rest.

At the same time, make a list of any items you wished you had taken, so that you can add these next time. Soon you should get your kit down to the minimum weight possible.

### TENTS
Single-skin tunnel tents made of waterproof, breathable material with a minimal frame of flexible poles are lightweight but pricey. Even lighter are bivvy bags, which dispense with a frame and simply form a waterproof covering for your sleeping bag.

Although lightweight tents can be strong and robust you will need to be careful, especially with the tent's groundsheet, which is likely to be very thin. If you pitch on a sharp piece of wood or rock you may damage it. One way around this is to place your sleeping mat on the ground before you pitch the tent over it, so you can still have the warmth of the mat to lie on but your groundsheet will be protected.

## COOKING EQUIPMENT

If you are a really lightweight camper, your cooking equipment will be very basic, which means that you will have to choose your food and utensils carefully, perhaps cutting the latter down to just a knife and a spoon.

If you are cooking on a single stove and using dehydrated foods, make sure you will have enough cooking pots. Choose a pan with a close-fitting lid that will double as a frying pan. Remember to check on the cooking times of packaged food: the longer the cooking time, the more fuel you will need. If you are going to carry food, take it out of its outer packaging but keep the cooking instructions.

Each of these things individually may save only grams/ounces, but added together they represent a significant weight saving.

▲ *Choosing a site with a good view may mean that it is exposed. Be sure that your lightweight tent will withstand the wind.*

▼ *If you have to pitch your tent on very stony ground, protect your groundsheet with your sleeping mat.*

### LIGHTWEIGHT EQUIPMENT

For a three-day trek in a temperate climate it should be possible to take the following gear per person without exceeding 9kg/20lb:
- Shirt, trousers, socks, underwear
- Fabric or leather walking boots
- Windproof jacket
- Woollen or fleece sweater
- Waterproof jacket and trousers
- Hat and gloves
- One-person tent, or bivvy bag and groundsheet
- Sleeping bag and insulated mat
- Lightweight backpack
- Canister stove and lighter
- Cooking fuel
- Cooking pot/mug and lid
- Spoon and knife
- Water bottles and purifier
- Food and food storage bag
- Whistle
- Wristwatch
- Map
- Compass
- First-aid kit
- Basic survival kit
- Sunglasses and sunscreen
- Insect repellent
- Wash kit

# Alternative Shelters

There may be occasions when you either do not have a tent or you are unable to use the tent you have, but you still need a shelter to protect yourself from the elements. A tent groundsheet can be used to form a makeshift shelter, or you could construct an A-frame shelter from tree branches; in snow conditions you could build a trench; alternatively, you could use natural landforms as shelter.

When choosing the site for a natural shelter, consider whether the ground will be waterlogged if it rains heavily. Cover the floor with a layer of bracken, ferns, heather or any other vegetation available. This will insulate you from the ground and will make you more comfortable; use only dry vegetation and shake it first to get rid of insects.

## GROUNDSHEET SHELTER

If you have a groundsheet, or a sheet of ripstop nylon, and a length of cord, tie the cord between two trees about 3m/10ft apart, and place the sheet over the cord. Then take the corners of the sheet and either peg them into the ground or tie a guy line to each corner and guy them out. This will provide you with the simplest of shelters, but it will be considerably better than a night in the open air, especially in windy or rainy conditions. Make sure the sheet comes down to 45–60cm/ 18–24in from the ground, or driving rain will soak you. The bivvy bag included in the survival kit can also be used as an emergency shelter if a groundsheet is not available. On its own, a bivvy bag can be used as a waterproof cover for a sleeping bag, but if you fix short tent poles or stout tree branches at its entrance, you can form a porch that effectively turns the bivvy bag into a small tent for one person.

## A-SHAPED NATURAL SHELTER

If you do not have a groundsheet big enough to make a shelter, find two convenient trees and rest a long branch or piece of wood between them, about 1.2m/4ft from the ground. Make sure you secure it very well, using either cord or natural vines, so that it will take the weight of the frame you are going to build.

Now lean some tree branches on the long branch at 30–45cm/12–18in intervals to form an A-shaped shelter. Fill in the gaps of the structure with

## BUILDING A GROUNDSHEET SHELTER

**1** Look for a fallen branch and place it between two trees about 1.2m/4ft from the ground, wedging it into the trunks or securing it with cord or rope.

**2** Unpack the groundsheet of your tent (or use your bivvy bag or space blanket) and throw it over the suspended branch.

**3** Arrange the groundsheet so that it hangs over both sides of the branch, coming down at least 45–60cm/ 18–24in off the ground on each side.

**4** Take one corner of the groundsheet and peg it out with a tent peg, or guy it with a guy line, or weight it down with a heavy log or rock.

**5** Work around the other three corners, securing the groundsheet firmly in place with tent pegs, guy lines, or heavy logs or rocks.

**6** With the four corners secured, the completed shelter will provide basic but effective protection from driving wind, rain or snow, or from an intense sun.

bracken, ferns or large leaves, starting at the bottom and working up, in the same way that a roof is tiled. If it rains, the rain will run down and off the sides and will not seep inside.

Alternatively, if there are pieces of plastic, wood or other materials around, you can use these to form the sides of the shelter. Do not use heavy pieces unless you can secure them, or else they may collapse on top of you.

### USING NATURAL LANDFORMS
In hot, dry areas, use natural landforms such as caves, overhangs or sand dunes to give you shelter from the sun and wind. Dry-stone walls can also be used as the basis for a shelter. Place tree branches diagonally from the top of the wall to the ground in front about 1m/3ft away, then cover the tree branches with whatever vegetation is available, or with your bivvy bag or a groundsheet. Make sure the wall is stable and is not likely to fall on you while you are inside the shelter.

### SNOW SHELTERS
If the snow is deep and you have tools such as a snow saw, machete or long knife with you, and you want the shelter to last for several days, you can build an igloo. For less permanent shelters to give protection from the elements, such as during a snowstorm or while the group takes a rest, you can dig a cave into a bank of snow or a trench in an open space.

---

#### LIVING IN SNOW

- Always make sure there is good ventilation inside your snow shelter, especially if the shelter is to be used by several people. Carbon dioxide will build up without adequate ventilation, and this can be fatal.
- Heat from your body will rise to the top of the shelter, while cold air will sink to ground level. Build a snow bench or platform inside the shelter so that you can sit or even sleep in the relatively pleasant warmer air.

---

### Igloo
To make an igloo, cut blocks 1m/3ft long, 40cm/15in high and 20cm/8in deep from one area of hard snow, using a snow saw, machete or long knife. Form a circle with the blocks around the hole from where the snow was cut, then build up the walls, overlapping and shaping the blocks so that they curve inwards. Cut a hole under one of the blocks for the cold air to seep out and for the entrance, then lay blocks along one wall inside the igloo to form a bench. The last block must be larger than the gap in the roof it has to fill. Place it on top of the igloo, then, from the inside, shape it into position so that it fills the gap exactly. Finally, cut ventilation holes through the walls, using an ice axe, machete, ski poles, or a stripped tree branch. In temperatures below freezing, the igloo will last for several days.

### Snow cave
If you need shelter but do not have the tools or the energy to build an igloo, hollow out a snow bank, using a shovel, if you have one, or your hands. This is the quickest way to take shelter from high winds and freezing temperatures. Block up the entrance behind you with roughly constructed lumps of snow. Poke a hole in the blocked-up entrance for ventilation, using an ice axe, ski pole or stripped tree branch.

▲ *In a desert environment, a shelter constructed from branches and vegetation will provide essential shade.*

### Snow trench
Open, flat spaces offer no natural protection from the elements in the way of trees, walls or hillsides. If you find yourself in need of shelter and you are equipped with a shovel, you can dig into the ground and build a snow trench. The deeper you dig, the more protection the trench will offer. If tree branches are available, make a roof by laying branches over the top; if you have time, you can lash the branches together using rope, cord or vegetation. Pack snow on to the frame, and poke a tree branch, ski pole or the shovel handle through the snow to make air holes. A bivvy bag can be laid over the top if tree branches are not available.

### Tree hollow shelter
If you are in a coniferous forest, the natural hollows at the base of the trees will make good temporary shelters. If the tree branches are laden with snow, take care not to dislodge the snow, as it is extremely heavy and will fall on you with an impact. Build a snow bench above the level of the floor to sleep or sit on, as the cold air will sink to the lowest point in the shelter, leaving you in warmer air. Always make sure there is good ventilation.

# Camp Safety and Hygiene

When camping, you should be even more aware of safety and hygiene than you are at home, particularly if you are in some remote area where help may be hard to summon. For this reason, all camp members should prioritize their own and each other's health and safety.

### TIDINESS

A basic rule to go by is that a tidy camp is a safe camp. On this basis, always try to have as much as possible packed away before you go to sleep each night, leaving out only those things that you may need during the night and first thing the next morning.

Never leave axes, knives or saws lying on the ground at any time, as someone could seriously hurt themselves if they fell on or over one of these. Keep all tools stored away when not in use: apart from the safety issue, this means that everyone will know where to find them. Finally, never tie a rope or washing line between trees in a position where someone is likely to walk into it. At night, mark any such line by putting something light-coloured over it.

### FIRE SAFETY

If you are cooking on a wood fire, make sure your woodpile is safe and that your fire cannot spread from the fire area. Use an existing fire pit if there is one on your campsite, and be very careful not to start a forest or brush fire in dry weather. Keep a bucket of sand or soil near the camp fire to use as a fire extinguisher in an emergency.

If you are cooking on a gas stove, do not cook in a sleeping tent and make sure that all gas is stored away from fires and sleeping areas and out of direct sunlight. Never change a gas cylinder in a confined space, and never put an empty cylinder on a fire.

When you eventually strike camp and put the fire out, make sure it is completely extinguished before leaving.

### HYGIENE AND SAFETY TIPS

- Whatever task you are doing in camp, tidy up as you go along.
- If you are leaving camp do not leave open fires, stoves or gaslights alight and unattended.
- If cooking in the porch of your tent make sure you have a good level area for your stove.
- Try not to eat food in a sleeping tent as crumbs and scraps will attract animals and insects.
- Keep all drinking water covered and mark it clearly to differentiate it from non-drinking water.
- Store all inflammables well away from fires and out of direct sunlight. Do not store fuel in sleeping tents.

▼ *In a large camp, pitch tents with enough space between them so that walkways are clear of guy lines and tent pegs.*

▲ *The highest standard of hygiene should be maintained when preparing food in camp. Dispose of kitchen waste scrupulously.*

## FOOD PREPARATION

Allocate a specific area of the camp site for the preparation of food and keep it scrupulously clean. Always wash your hands in clean, purified water before preparing food and wash dishes and utensils promptly to avoid attracting flies. In hot weather, cook and eat fresh food such as fish as quickly as possible

▼ *If you are sleeping out, do not sleep too near a camp fire in case you roll on to it during the night, or sparks fly on to you.*

after bringing it into camp, and don't keep cooked food standing around cooling, as bacteria will proliferate.

## WASTE DISPOSAL

Dispose of all waste food by burning and burying it as soon as possible (see the section Base Camps). If you cannot bury it, pack it into a plastic bag and put it in a bin as soon as possible. Never store waste near the sleeping area, and never leave food uncovered because it will attract wild animals.

## TENT HYGIENE

If you are camping in the same area for more than one night, try to keep your tents tidy, clean and aired, if the weather allows. If your tents do not have sewn-in groundsheets, lift the walls each day to air them. If they do have sewn-in groundsheets, open the doors and sweep out the tents each day. Turn your sleeping bag inside out and air it for an hour or so each day, preferably in the sun. Afterwards roll it up until you need it so that nothing can crawl into it before you do.

## TOILETS AND WASHING

Dig a hole or latrine for solid waste and cover it with soil each time it is used. Have a separate urination point. To make sure the used water from your washing area cannot run straight into a river or lake, dig a soakaway channel so that the dirty water will be filtered through the ground first.

▲ *When using chopping or cutting tools make sure you have no obstacles or people around you who might get hurt.*

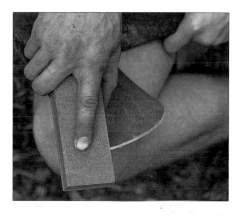

▲ *Keep your wood-chopping axe sharp with a Carborundum stone: a sharp blade is safer than a blunt one.*

▼ *Always cook outside a tent, though you can use the porch to shelter the stove, and never store stove fuel inside a sleeping tent.*

## TINDER AND KINDLING

To make a camp fire you need tinder and kindling as well as fuel. Tinder and kindling have separate functions. Tinder is used as a firestarter, to kick-start the burning of kindling, which in turn is used to ignite the fuel. Lighted kindling on its own could be used to light fuel, but setting the kindling alight first with tinder means that you need much less of a flame initially to start the camp fire fuel burning. This could be important in wet or humid conditions or where you are finding it difficult to light a flame.

### Tinder

Any material can be used as tinder so long as it is highly combustible, and the best tinder will need only a spark to set it alight. Avoid using highly flammable materials such as aerosol spray cans, as these can explode when ignited and the explosion will be difficult to control.

If you know you will be building your own camp fire and you cannot guarantee the weather will be sunny and dry for the duration of your trip, it is a good idea to take your own tinder with you, storing it in a small waterproof container so that it doesn't get wet in a heavy shower. This will ensure that you always have a supply to hand whenever you need it.

▲ *So long as it is absolutely dry, crisp leaf litter makes excellent kindling for a fire; pine needles and dry grass are alternatives.*

▲ *Pine cones can be used as fuel if dry, and are worth collecting if they are plentiful, but they do not burn particularly well.*

▲ *Twigs and small branches make ideal kindling providing they are dry. Break them into a manageable size before use.*

▲ *Dry bark found on the forest floor can be used as kindling. Do not strip bark from trees because it can cause considerable damage.*

Manmade tinder materials can be bought from outdoor suppliers, but there are many natural materials that are readily available – free of charge – outdoors. Keep an eye out for new tinder supplies as you follow your route, even if you do not need them that day. If the weather is dry you can store the materials in a waterproof container until needed. In wet weather you can dry damp materials inside your tent or at the side of the camp fire – not so close that they catch fire – until they are dry enough to be stored.

### Kindling

Materials used for kindling are types of wood. The best materials are small, dry twigs and sticks. The soft woods flare up quicker than hard woods (those that contain resin burn particularly well), but they can produce sparks and will burn very fast, which means that you may need more of them to light a large camp fire. Kindling should be bigger than tinder in order to encourage a high flame, but it should be smaller than the fuel wood, so that it can be packed between the pieces of fuel.

### SOURCES OF TINDER

- Silver birch bark
- Crushed dry, fallen tree leaves
- Crushed dry, fallen fir cones
- Dry, fallen pine needles
- Dry, fallen seed heads
- Short lengths of dried grass
- Any plant down
- Fine wood or bark shavings
- Bird down
- Dried, powdered fungi
- Short newspaper strips
- Short waxed paper strips
- Short strips of rubber car tyre
- Cotton wool
- Camera film
- Cotton fluff from clothing
- Charred natural fabric, such as cotton or silk

### FIRE STICKS

Firesticks are kindling that has been "feathered" to make it catch fire more quickly. To prepare a firestick from a dry twig, make small shallow cuts down the length of the twig with a knife. Then tease out the fronds so that they bend outwards to catch the flame more easily.

Avoid collecting kindling straight from the ground as it will be damp and will take longer to burn. Carry it with you in a waterproof container if possible; if you have to use damp wood as kindling, shave off the outside and use the inner part, which will be dry.

### Using tinder and kindling

When your camp fire is ready to light, ignite the tinder using a match, lighter, artificial flint striker or traditional flint and steel. When it is burning, hold the tinder against the kindling. As the flame takes hold and rises, pack the kindling in between pieces of fuel wood on the camp fire, which should start to burn.

## CHOOSING WOOD

If you are planning to use a camp fire to cook your meals, you will be relying significantly on wood as your fuel supply, so find out as much as you can about the burning properties of the wood available in the area before you travel. Know how to identify the wood you need, and make sure you are equipped with the right tools to deal with it.

Some woods, such as telegraph poles and treated fencing or building timbers, are dangerous to burn because they contain chemicals that give off a toxic smoke: do not use these even if you see them lying on the ground and are sure they are unwanted debris. Natural woods can also be unsuitable: bamboo can trap water in its stems, and this may explode when heated on the fire.

Different woods burn in different ways. Some burn faster than others and produce varying amounts of heat, making them particularly suited to different methods of cooking – those that burn quickly are better for boiling and those that burn slowly and give out a lot of heat are better for roasting. Knowing the character of your wood fuel will help you to use it in a more efficient way, reducing the quantity of fuel you need and the amount of time spent sourcing it. Be prepared to use different types of wood on your fire if you plan to boil some ingredients and roast others for the same meal.

Hard woods are generally regarded as the best woods for roasting or grilling foods because they burn hot and for a long time (avoid using willow unless it is very dry because it has a high water content and therefore burns poorly). Soft woods burn quickly and for a shorter amount of time, and are best used for boiling.

Whatever the type of wood, it must be dead and well dried if it is to burn well (one exception is ash, which burns well whether it is dry or green). Wood picked from the ground will be damp, and this will burn with an unpleasant amount of smoke and not enough heat (the fire's energy is used up drying out the wood). Instead, look for dead wood that is caught up in branches: a vertical position means it will be drier.

## HARD WOODS

▲ *Apple and cherry burn well and give off a pleasant and sweet smell. They grow in sunny areas of temperate climates.*

▲ *Holly is found in woodland areas in temperate and cold, dry climates. Holly and yew burn equally well whether green or dry.*

▲ *Narrow-leaved ash usually grows in wet temperate conditions so it will need to be well dried before it can be burned.*

▲ *The silver birch grows in mountainous regions of temperate climates. It lights easily and the bark makes good kindling.*

## SOFT WOODS

▲ *Cedars and other coniferous trees make excellent kindling and good fire fuel, giving out a lot of heat.*

▲ *Horse chestnut is common to cooler temperate climates. Like all softwoods, it burns quickly and gives out a lot of light.*

▲ *Small-leaved lime is common to warm temperate and hot, dry climates. It is not easy to light but will give off a good heat.*

▲ *Cones from spruce and any other coniferous tree can be used as a fuel but will not burn with much of a flame.*

# Useful Knots

The following knots have been found to be useful for life in the wilderness. It is a good idea to practise them so that they can be tied as second nature. They are designed to be tied with natural fibre rope, and may not be as successful with synthetic ropes.

## FISHERMAN'S KNOT OR WATER KNOT

This is used to join two ends of a rope together to form a loop, such as a sling, or to tie two ropes of similar thickness together. It is not secure enough to be used for tying climbing ropes together, or any ropes that are to bear a heavy weight.

**1** Lay the two lines parallel, tying an overhand knot with one end around the standing part of the other. Turn the half-completed knot end-for-end.

**2** Tie an identical overhand knot with the other end. Pull first on both ends to tighten the knots, then on the standing parts to tighten the knot.

## BOWLINE

This creates a non-slip knot in a rope. It can be used to make a loop at the end of a rope, or a waist loop for a climbing rope, when you do not have a climbing harness.

To make it more secure, once you have tied the knot, finish it off with two half hitches. It can become less secure if the rope is very stiff, or wet and slippery.

**1** Bring the working end across the standing part of the rope to form an overhand loop.

**2** Rotate the hand clockwise and so produce a smaller loop in the standing part of the rope.

**3** Ensure that the working end points upwards, from back to front, through the smaller loop.

**4** Lead the end behind the standing part, then tuck it back down through the small loop from front to back.

**5** Arrange the bowline with a long end (longer than shown) and secure further, if necessary, with tape or a half hitch.

## CLOVE HITCH

This can be used to suspend a light object at right angles to the suspension point or to tie a boat to a pole. The pull of the clove hitch must be steady, because the knot can work loose if it is not under tension. It can also jam if it becomes wet. If the knot has to last for any length of time, tie the two ends together to secure it more permanently.

**1** Hold the rope in a straight line and make an overhand loop of any size at any convenient point in the line.

**2** Add an underhand loop further along the line, so that there is now a pair of loops consisting of two opposing halves.

**3** Arrange the two loops so that they are the same size and close together in the line of rope.

**4** Rotate the two loops a little, at the same time, in opposite directions, in order to position them so that they overlap precisely.

**5** Insert the rail, spar, rope or other foundation through both of the loops and pull on either one or both ends to tighten the resulting hitch.

## ROUND TURN AND TWO HALF HITCHES

This is a strong and secure knot or hitch, which can be used to secure a rope to a pole or ring, tow a broken-down vehicle or secure the guy lines of a tent. It will even make a haulage knot for securing a load or climbing. Before you trust a heavy weight to the knot, check the condition of the rope: if it feels soft and amenable, it is worn out and should not be used.

**1** Take a turn around the anchorage of the pole or ring and bring the working end alongside the standing part. Apply a single half hitch by tying an overhand knot with the working end of the rope.

**2** Add an identical second half hitch and draw the two snugly together to complete this dependable knot.

## SIMPLE SIMON OVER

This knot is good for general camping use. It is especially effective in slick synthetic lines and, once mastered, it can be tied easily. It has rarely appeared in print, but it merits being more widely known as it is a secure knot and a very useful one to have at your disposal when faced with tying slippery, synthetic lines in a howling gale out in the field.

**1** Make a bight in one of the two lines to be joined. Bring the working end of the other line over it. Tuck the working end down through the bight.

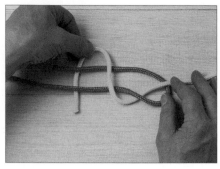

**2** Bring the working end out to the left (in this instance), then take it over both bight legs and, in a snaking "Z" track, back again beneath them.

**3** Lay the end back over its preceeding part (the "over" of the knot name).

**4** From the outside of the bight, tuck the working end up and through and finally lay it alongside its own standing part. Tighten, working the slack out.

## SIMPLE SIMON UNDER

This is a variation of the Simple Simon Over knot, above. It is more secure than the Over knot and it will cope better with dissimilar cord sizes and textures. To make the Under knot, first complete steps 1 and 2 of the Over knot.

**1** After bringing the working end of the line back beneath both bight legs, tuck it beneath its preceding part (the "under" of the knot name).

**2** From the outside of the bight, tuck the working end up through and finally lay it alongside its own standing part. Slowly work the slack out of the knot.

## VICE VERSA

Some intractable materials – such as wet and slimy leather thongs or bungee (elastic) shock cord – are difficult to keep in place and will slither out of other bends. The Vice Versa is one way to keep these kinds of rope lines securely in place. The various tucks and turns that make up this knot are the secret of its very reliable strength and security.

**1** Lay the two lines to be joined parallel and together.

**2** Take the working end of the line on the right-hand side and bring it beneath the other standing part.

**3** Pass the end over the other line and then tuck it beneath itself.

**4** Take the other working end on the left-hand side, passing over the first of the two lines. Now bring the second working end back beneath the other line and up past the front of the knot (with no tuck).

**5** Cross the right-hand end over the left-hand end and tuck it through the left-hand loop alongside its own standing part. Similarly, take hold of what has become the right-hand end. Tuck the remaining working end through the right-hand loop alongside its own standing part. Gently pull on all four emerging lines at once to securely tighten this knot.

# Using an Axe

Axes are useful for cutting down trees, removing branches and cutting up timber. As long as the axe is sharp and in good working order and you are aware of the dangers, accidents should not happen. Dress appropriately, with jackets and shirts fastened up to avoid them flapping around and getting caught, and wear strong footwear; do not wear open-toed sandals or bare feet.

Trees should never be felled or branches lopped unless you have the express permission of the landowner.

### MAINTENANCE
Sharpen a blunt axe on a Carborundum stone, which can be used either wet or dry. Replace a split handle and check the axe head to see that the wedge is tightly fitted in and there are no chips out of the blade. After use, clean the blade and cover it before storing.

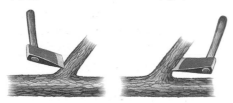

▼ *When cutting branches from the trunk of a tree, start from the base and work upwards (left); do not work downwards (right).*

▼ *When chopping a log, weaken the log with a V-shaped cut by first making one cut from the right and one from the left.*

▼ *Never be tempted to use your foot to secure a log you are about to cut. If the axe slips it could result in a very serious injury. Safety is paramount at all times.*

▲ *Carry an axe with the blade in the palm of your hand, facing outwards and away from your body in case you should fall over.*

### CLOTHING
Make sure your clothes are neat as loose clothing could get caught as you swing the axe. Protect your feet with leather walking boots or walking shoes; you should not have bare feet or wear flip-flops or open-toed sandals.

### PREPARATION
Before starting work, clear the area all around, including smaller overhead branches, or the axe may catch. Check that the ground you are standing on is firm and clear of obstacles. Make sure that nobody is within at least two axe-plus-arm lengths away from you. This is not just to avoid hitting someone but also to avoid wood chips flying up into their eyes as you chop.

### CHOPPING DOWN A TREE
Decide where you want the tree to fall, and make a cut facing in that direction. On the other side of the tree, start to cut through the tree above the first cut. Remove any low branches that can be easily reached on the side away from the direction of fall, chopping parallel to the trunk rather than towards it. This should encourage the tree to fall

▲ *You should always wear stout footwear and close-fitting clothes when working with an axe or any other sharp tool.*

in the correct direction. When the tree is about to fall, shout "Timber!" and move to one side, so you will not be caught by the bottom of the tree swinging back or up. You can also use your axe for cutting and splitting the tree trunk into logs.

▼ *Make sure you have a clear area around you before starting to use an axe to chop logs, in case of any flying wood chips.*

# Using a Saw

Saws can be used for any wood-cutting job, and they do not leave the same amount of wasteful wood chips and debris as an axe. A high level of safety is required, as with an axe, because a saw has the potential to be a highly dangerous instrument.

### MAINTENANCE

Before use, check to see that the blade is tight in the handle and that the teeth are sharp. Check from time to time that the teeth are not becoming clogged with wood shavings or resin from the wood. After use, clean the blade to remove wood shavings, and pack it away clean and dry. Keep the saw well oiled or greased to prevent rust. When not in use, mask the blade, either by using a plastic clip or mask or by tying a length of robust sacking around the saw several times.

### CLOTHING

Wear jackets and shirts buttoned up and generally avoid wearing loose items of clothing, as the teeth of a saw could easily catch in them. Sturdy gloves will protect your hands in the case of the saw slipping, and may make it easier to grip the wood; mittens restrict your fingers and will not give you a firm enough grip.

### TRIMMING A TREE

A saw can be used for cutting up small timber and is ideal for trimming a tree before or after it has been felled. Trim

▼ *When felling a tree the first, lower cut needs to be made on the side on which you want the tree to fall.*

the tree from the bottom and work upwards. Hold the tree with a tight grip, keeping your fingers well away from the moving blade.

### FELLING A TREE

Make the first cut in the direction you want the tree to fall, then make the second cut on the opposite side of the tree, above the first cut. Work slowly until the blade has made a good deep cut in the wood. If at any time you feel tired, stop for a break. If you are using a two-handed or two-person saw, put your main effort into the pull stroke.

▲ *Rest the timber you are cutting on a secure base and get someone to hold it if necessary: never try to saw on the ground.*

Once you are about a quarter of the way through, push above the saw cut to take the pressure off the blade. If the saw blade jams, do not force the blade out. If necessary, take the blade out of the saw handle and work it out slowly, using a little oil or grease.

▼ *When two people are using a saw together, each of them should only ever cut on the pull stroke.*

# Planning your Outdoor Kitchen

If you are a lightweight camper, your kitchen will be little more than a fire or stove sited a little way from your tent. If you are establishing a camp on one site for more than a week, however, it will be worth planning the layout of your camp kitchen, and you may even want to build some simple structures to make your life easier.

### ESTABLISHING THE COOKING AREA

The first thing to do is to fence the cooking area off in some way so that people cannot just wander through it unawares and get in the way of the cook. If there are children in the camp you may want some way of deterring them from getting too near the stove or helping themselves to the food while you are preparing it. Your store tent and woodpile, and any structures you build for the kitchen area, will all help to establish its boundaries.

Next, choose where you are going to put your cooking site, be this a stove or fire. If there is a suitable natural feature such as a flat rock, use this as your base; otherwise, if you can, build a framework off the ground as the base for the fire, so that when you are cooking you will not have to bend over all the time. Make sure this framework is substantial and

▲ *A safe cooking fire is spacious and well thought out. Large timbers around the fire provide both a safety barrier and seating.*

will not wobble or collapse once you have built the fire and loaded it with cooking pots. Allow some space for the cooks to stand. If you are using a fire, keep the woodpile well stocked, but make sure it is kept tidy, as leaving pieces of wood around could cause people to trip over them.

You will need to put your store tent near the cooking area, but don't have it so near that it gets in the way of the people doing the cooking.

### PROTECTING THE KITCHEN

You may choose to build one or two structures in the kitchen area to keep eating and cooking equipment off the ground. If you construct a simple table you can use it to prepare all your food and also as a serving area, and some form of dresser will keep the cooking equipment tidy and help to demarcate the kitchen area. If your campsite has trees growing

◀ *In a long-term base camp the kitchen will be easier to organize if you can set up some kind of dresser to keep all your cooking equipment together and off the ground.*

around it, they can be useful in several ways, though you should not build your fire or site your stove too close to them. Leafy trees will provide shade for keeping food cool, and in a hot climate they will also offer welcome shade for the cook, to offset the heat of the fire. You can also use any branches within reach as racks on which to hang utensils, mugs and food. It makes sense to store as much off the ground as you can, to keep things clean and make them easier to find, and to clear the area where you are preparing food.

### THE EATING AREA

In a large camp it's a good idea to establish a designated eating area to help keep the rest of the site tidy and free of food debris. If you are in a place where it rains regularly, you might consider it a good idea to have a shelter over both your fire and the eating area. Discourage people from eating in their tents as crumbs and spilt food may act as a lure for animals later on. You will need to dig two waste pits near the kitchen (see the section Base Camps) or have two bags, one for dry waste and one for wet waste. Insist that everyone disposes of all waste responsibly.

▲ *A mug tree is useful for keeping mugs clean and organized. On a campsite it can be the branch of an actual tree.*

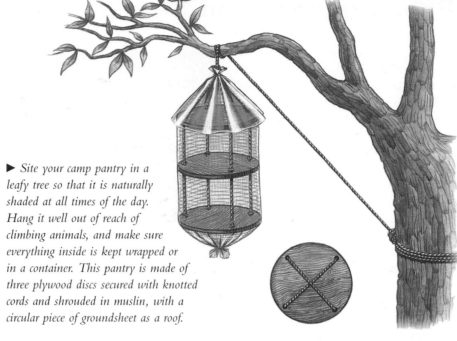

▶ *Site your camp pantry in a leafy tree so that it is naturally shaded at all times of the day. Hang it well out of reach of climbing animals, and make sure everything inside is kept wrapped or in a container. This pantry is made of three plywood discs secured with knotted cords and shrouded in muslin, with a circular piece of groundsheet as a roof.*

### THE CAMP PANTRY

If you have a store tent, all dry and packaged food can be kept in it, but fresh food will need to be kept as cool as possible. For this you can use a hanging camp pantry. You can buy these in various styles, but you can also make one with a few pieces of wood, a length of muslin (cheesecloth) or nylon mesh, and some cord. Hang the pantry from a rope slung over the

▼ *By constructing a fire or stove stand you will save yourself a lot of bending down, but you must make sure that it is very stable and will not collapse when loaded with fuel and heavy cooking pots.*

branch of a large tree and make sure it stays in the shade for as much of the day as possible. Any food that you keep inside it should be well wrapped up or packed in an airtight container.

### BEAR BAGGING

In case the camp is visited by animals attracted by the smell of your fresh food, the pantry and any other bags containing food should be hung far enough away from the trunk of the tree to prevent them climbing to get to it. This is particularly important if you are camping in bear country. Unless you can hang your food around 4m/13ft high and 3m/10ft away from the trunk you may lose it all to a hungry bear. You should also hang food downwind of your camp so that if any bears do want to investigate it they don't need to pass you to get to it.

To rig up your bag or pantry, weight the end of a rope with a small rock tied into a bag and toss it over a high branch, keeping hold of the other end. Lower the rope until you can reach the rock, which you can discard. Tie your food

bag to one end of the rope and use the other end to haul it up to a suitable height. Make the end of the rope fast around the tree trunk.

If you are camping in an area with no trees, this arrangement will not be an option for you. In this case, try to avoid the need to store fresh food at all by taking dehydrated, pouch or canned food supplies instead. If you do have to keep fresh food at ground level, use thick double wrapping to mask the smell of the food, and avoid any particularly smelly foods if you don't want to risk attracting animals to your camp. Pack the food in sealable plastic containers and don't keep it inside or around your sleeping tent.

▼ *Empty food cans should be cleaned out or burned, then squashed and taken away from the site when you leave, or buried at least 90cm/3ft underground.*

# Food Hygiene and Storage

You will be faced with many hazards in the wild, so the last thing you should do is add to them by failing to practise sound food hygiene. If you are part of a group, bear in mind that everyone's health depends on the whole group taking equal care in this respect. If any members of an expedition do not follow the basic rules of food safety, they risk causing bouts of diarrhoea or even a serious case of food poisoning.

### FOOD PREPARATION
Make sure that anybody preparing or cooking food washes their hands

▼ *You should have separate chopping boards for different types of food to prevent any cross-contamination.*

▲ *Be scrupulous about washing your hands before you start to prepare food, whether it is to be eaten raw or cooked.*

▲ *All the plates, cups and bowls from which you eat should be properly washed in hot water after each use.*

frequently. Keep raw and cooked foods separate during preparation, and, if possible, use different chopping boards and utensils for each type. If you cannot do this, make sure they are thoroughly washed before changing from one type of food to the other. For more advice on the preparation of food, see the section Local Foods.

### CLEANLINESS
Cooking pans, plates, cups and cutlery must be washed thoroughly in hot water after each meal, and with antiseptic added to the water every three or four days, if possible. To cut down the possibility of spreading infection, each person should use only their own eating equipment and drink from their own mug or water bottle.

In a base camp or semi-permanent camp kitchen, use an antibacterial fluid to clean all working surfaces and utensils at least every three or four days. In hot climates this

▲ *Make sure all your cooking equipment is thoroughly cleaned and disinfect everything every three or four days.*

should be done every day. Make sure that all dishcloths and drying towels are washed regularly.

Check that wooden cooking utensils are kept clean and in good condition. If they get chipped or badly scored, discard them and buy new ones as they are likely to harbour germs.

### SERVING FOOD
Well-cooked, piping hot food will be safe to eat, but if it is left to sit around at a lower temperature, bacteria will start to multiply. For this reason, if you are going to serve a lot of people, call them before you take the food off the fire, so that it is still very hot when it reaches their plates.

Serve each dish using a different spoon, if possible, and clean up any

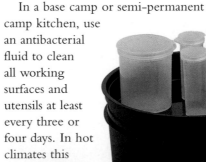

◀ *Specialized lightweight equipment is excellent for backpacking expeditions but may not be robust enough for use in a larger base camp.*

▲ *Although it is bulky, a large plastic bowl for washing dishes will be useful in camp.*

▲ *Collapsible mesh covers are invaluable for keeping flies off dishes of food.*

▲ *A weighted fabric cover can be used to protect dishes of all sizes from flies.*

spillages as soon as they happen. If you have to touch any prepared foods – including bread – wash your hands first: this applies whether you are serving it or picking it up to eat.

Finally, keep all food covered until you are ready to serve it, and, if the food is cold, get it ready and serve it in the shade.

### DRY FOOD STORAGE

All items should be stored in a cool, dry, well-ventilated place, raised off the ground. Try to make sure your storage is bird- and rodent-proof and never leave food containers open. If you do not have a lid for a pot use a piece of muslin (cheesecloth) to cover it.

▼ *Proper serving implements, such as ladles and large spoons, are essential if you are catering for a large camp.*

No food should be kept in a sleeping tent at a base camp. If you are on a lightweight camping trip this is less easy to arrange, but you should pack all your food away in containers or put it in your backpack.

If you buy dried fish or meat from local traders in tropical countries, make sure you wash it well before eating it. It may well have been dried out in the sun, which will have allowed flies and other insects to settle on it.

### FRESH AND COOKED FOOD STORAGE

Unless you are cooking in a semi-permanent base camp and have some form of refrigeration or effective cool boxes, do not keep either fresh or cooked foods for long periods, and never for more than 24 hours in a hot country. Keep all food out of the sun

and covered with muslin to keep flies away, and never store cooked and uncooked food together.

If you are camping within reach of local markets or food producers, try and buy all your fresh food daily, then you can cook it straight away and storing it will not be a problem.

As an alternative to going to the market, you may have local traders coming to your camp or base. If you want to use this arrangement, make sure you stipulate a time and place, as you will not want a succession of people turning up throughout the day trying to sell you food.

If you can, try to spread your purchases around a number of different traders when you are visiting a Third World country. Your money will make a big difference to small farmers and traders in the locality.

### SERVING MEALS

- As well as the cooks, people serving food must have the highest standards of cleanliness, both personally and with the equipment they are using.
- Serving food should not be a free-for-all. Either ask everyone to sit down and serve them where they are going to eat or get them to queue up so that you can serve the food on to their plates: don't let them use their own spoons.
- Make sure all your serving equipment is clean and you use a separate implement for each pan.

# Cooking over a Fire

Most cooking is more successful when it is done on a good bed of hot embers rather than over a fire with lots of flames. So this means preparing the fire by burning a good amount of fuel until it has died down to a bed of embers, then placing your pots safely either directly on the fire or on its surrounds.

## HEAVY-DUTY POTS

Use heavy-duty cooking pots when cooking on a fire. If your pots and pans are too thin and flimsy they will not heat evenly and the food inside is likely to burn. The fire may also damage the cooking pots themselves, especially if you are cooking directly on the fire. If you have constructed a structure to support the pots (see the section Camp Fires), they will be exposed to less intense heat.

Have a padded oven glove or something similar to lift pots off the fire, as the handles may become very hot. Be careful when lifting pots on or off the fire that you do not get smoke in your eyes, as this could lead you to drop the pot.

If a pot is extremely heavy, use two people to lift it off the fire and warn others in the cooking area to get out of the way while you are doing so.

### PROTECTING COOKWARE

If planning to cook on open fires, coat the outside of cooking pots with a paste made up of washing powder and water, and allow it to dry before putting the pots on the fire. When you come to wash the pots, this coating will wash off with the layer of soot on it.

▲ *Make sure the pot is completely stable when you put it on the fire, and will not fall over during cooking.*

You may lift the pot by pushing a stick through the handle with one person on each side, but if you use this method make sure the stick is strong enough and will not break when the full weight of the pan and contents is brought to bear.

On a windy day, be careful that ash from the fire does not blow into your cooking pots or food.

## PLANNING COOKING TIMES

Before you start cooking, think about the way you are going to use the fire: for instance, you may need access to the hottest part of the fire to grill some meat, while pots are simmering gently over a cooler part, so make sure you can reach everything easily. If you are cooking a meal with a number of different elements, consider which foods will take longest to cook, and start with these.

If you want to cook a number of dishes all at the same time, and have enough people, you can make one person responsible for each dish, making sure it is ready on time and does not burn.

## KEEPING EMBERS HOT

Once you have constructed your fire (see the section Camp Fires), and it is burning, don't forget it while you are cooking. If the bed of embers starts to cool down, you may have to stop cooking and burn some more wood. Since stopping the cooking process is

▼ *When you put a pan on the fire, try to arrange the handle so that it is shielded from the fiercest heat.*

▶ *Woodland will supply shelter and fuel for your camp fire, but be careful to choose a site for the fire that is not too near the trees.*

rarely ideal, a better solution is to use part of your fire, where you have the bed of embers, for cooking, and keep a wood-burning fire stoked on another part to create a steady supply of hot embers that you can rake across when you need them.

Make sure you have a good supply of wood for the fire, as you will not want to have to hunt for more wood halfway through cooking a meal.

## CAMP OVEN

If you have a camp oven, place it at one end of the fire and bank earth or sand around it to make it secure and keep it at a constant temperature. The door should face away from the fire so that food can be put in and taken out easily and safely.

Remember that, as in most ovens, the temperature will be higher in the upper part than in the bottom. You do not want fire directly under the oven, as this can turn the bottom of the oven into a hot plate and cause anything left on this to burn.

▼ *Let the fire die down to a bed of glowing, ash-covered embers before cooking on it, so that food cooks rather than burns.*

## COOKING IN THE CAMP FIRE

It can be great fun to cook a meal using the minimum of utensils, though this is not usually practicable if you are catering for a large number of people. With this type of cooking it is particularly important to have a good bed of embers and no flame on your cooking fire. You can use aluminium foil to keep food moist and protect it from burning on the outside, and from getting covered with ash.

You need to make sure that everything is cooked thoroughly when using this method. One secret is to cut everything into fairly small pieces or thin slices. If you are using ingredients such as potatoes or apples, try to cut them into pieces that are all of roughly the same size, so they cook evenly.

Be careful not to burn yourself when putting things on the fire, or taking them off.

## FIRE SAFETY

Make sure everyone using the camp fire follows these rules:
- Site the fire well away from trees and other vegetation.
- Never throw wood on a fire, but place it on gently.
- Always have water available in case you need to put it out.
- Never allow people to mess about around a fire, especially when it is being used for cooking.
- Keep the area around the fire clean and tidy.
- Keep the woodpile well clear of the fire.
- If you have pans of water or food on a fire make sure someone is looking after them.
- Use an oven glove or padded glove to take pans off the fire.

# Cooking on Stoves

If you are going to use a stove for cooking, you will need to decide how many burners you need, or even how many stoves if the party is a big one. A single-burner stove will be the lightest to carry, but meals will be limited and slow to prepare.

## USING STOVES SAFELY

Make sure you always operate a stove of any kind in a well-ventilated area and never store any fuel in or near a sleeping tent. This is especially important if you are using a gas stove. Never change a gas cylinder in a confined space or near a naked flame. If you need to remove it to dismantle the stove, leave it to cool first then take off the cylinder quickly and check that it has sealed itself and is not leaking.

A stove will not burn as hot as a fire, so you can use much lighter pans on it. If the stove is burning on full power,

▲ *Always set up your stove on a flat, stable surface to ensure that it will not tip over while it is in use.*

▲ *In windy conditions use a windshield, either a purpose-made one or something like a log, a rock or another piece of equipment.*

## USING A GAS STOVE

**1** Outside (not in a confined area) attach the gas cylinder to the burner.

**2** Light the stove by turning on the gas and applying a flame.

**3** Let the stove cool if dismantling it, and remove the cylinder quickly.

## USING A METHYLATED SPIRIT STOVE

**1** Assemble the stove and place it on a flat, level surface. Fill the burner.

**2** Carefully light the methylated spirit (methyl alcohol).

**3** Extinguish the flame by placing the screw top over the burner.

however, the food may still burn if you don't watch it carefully.

If it is very windy, either use your stove's windshield or improvise one using something from your kit or natural materials such as logs. Make sure you don't position anything so close to the stove that it catches light.

When you have finished cooking, turn the stove off. If you need to dismantle it, let it cool down before doing so, and give it a good clean before packing it away. If it requires special tools to maintain it, make sure they are packed with the stove for easy access when you need them.

## COOKING ON A SINGLE-BURNER STOVE

If you are backpacking and have just a single-burner stove, you will have to plan your cooking carefully, as you will not be able to cook anything that requires more than one pan per course.

Before you start cooking, make sure that your stove is in good working order with plenty of fuel. To avoid wasting any fuel, do all the food preparation before lighting the stove. Once the pan is on top, the stove may become top-heavy and unstable, so do not leave it unattended.

## COOKING ON A MULTI-BURNER STOVE

If you are cooking on a multi-burner stove, perhaps with a grill as well, you should be able to cook the sort of meals you do at home. Unless you have an oven in which to keep things hot, remember to plan your cooking so that all the different parts of the meal are ready at the same time.

Only the cooks should be around the stove and cooking area. This is particularly important if you are having to cook in a tent or confined space, where someone could kick or knock over the stove and food, which could be very dangerous.

▼ *A double-burner gas stove is a more efficient way to cater for a large group.*

▼ *The army mess tin is designed to be used with the army solid fuel stove.*

## USING A SOLID FUEL STOVE

**1** Open the can of fuel, remove the foil covering and assemble the stove.

**2** Light the fuel. If it is in gel form, be careful not to get any on your hands.

**3** Extinguish the flame using the lid and leave to cool before packing away.

## USING A PETROL STOVE

**1** Make sure the fuel tank is full and assemble the stove.

**2** Give the tank several pumps with the plunger and turn the valve.

**3** Light the stove. After cooking, turn off the burner and release the valve.

# Lightweight Camp Menus

If you are going to have to carry all your food on your back, in cycle panniers or in a canoe, your main concern is likely to be the lightness of your food rather than its variety. Nevertheless, after a week or so eating the same freeze-dried dishes, you may feel your priority was wrong. Beyond pre-packaged, freeze-dried meals there is plenty of lightweight food on supermarket shelves, and with a little imagination you can devise interesting and appetizing menus for each day.

When choosing your food, consider how many cooking pots and burners you will have to cook on. You should also take the time to read the cooking directions on the food packets. Some soups, for example, take just a few minutes to cook, whereas others can take 20 minutes, meaning that you will need to use (and carry) extra fuel.

### BREAKFAST

If you want to be up and on the move quickly, a bread roll with jam may be as much as you have time for. If you have a camp fire, the bread can be toasted over the fire. There are plenty of muesli (granola) and other cereals on the market that are ideal for a speedy breakfast, but for these you will need milk or yogurt. In cold weather you can warm yourself up with instant porridge (oatmeal), which can be mixed

*▼ If you use aluminium or enamel eating equipment be aware that they get very hot when filled with hot food.*

with either hot water or milk. You can buy it packed in individual portions for camping, and in different flavours such as cinnamon and apple or maple syrup and brown sugar.

If you want a more substantial cooked breakfast to keep you going through the day, you could heat a small can of beans, or beans with sausage, and eat that with bread. A more expensive option might be a suitable recipe in the form of a pouch meal.

Make sure you have plenty to drink at breakfast time. It doesn't matter if your drinks are hot or cold, but you could have hours ahead of you where you will be losing fluid by walking or working.

*◀ A mug of soup, hot baked beans and an instant pudding can be prepared using the smallest stove in just a few minutes and they make a warming and sustaining meal.*

### LUNCH

If you are on the move during the day you will probably want only a brief break at lunchtime and won't want to eat anything that will slow you down. Lunch will usually be in the form of a high-energy snack meal that will need very little preparation and will be easy to eat. Nuts, fruit, chocolate and energy bars are the sorts of foods that will give you this high energy but will not require the body to over-exert itself digesting them.

### DINNER

The evening meal will be your main meal of the day, when you have made camp at the end of your journey, or finished work. It should be a substantial three-course affair.

The first course can be a packet of instant soup, which just needs hot water poured on to it. The main course might be either a dehydrated meal or a pouch meal. If you're eating fish or meat, make sure you also have plenty of carbohydrates, in the form of rice, instant mashed potatoes or pasta, with it. All of these are easy to cook and light to carry.

The final course can be something like an instant pudding or fruit cooked with custard, both of which can be bought in dehydrated form. If you buy one of the varieties that just need hot water added to make them, you will save yourself the trouble of having to wash up one of the cooking pans you used for the main course.

## COOKING DEHYDRATED FOOD

- Do not eat dehydrated food without adding the correct amount of water: it will dehydrate you.
- Add extra water at high altitudes.
- Soak ingredients such as dried vegetables in the cooking water before you start to cook them, to improve rehydration.

- Cook over a gentle heat, and keep stirring as the food cooks to avoid burning.
- Taste before adding any salt, as some dry foods are very salty.
- Get water boiling before adding rice or pasta.
- Thicken liquids with instant potato mash, raw eggs, grated cheese or powdered milk added at the end of cooking.

◀ *Dried pasta is quick to cook and provides a substantial evening meal. Bring a pan of water to the boil and tip in the pasta. Leave to boil for about 12 minutes, stirring occasionally, then drain and add to your chosen sauce. Heat through and serve.*

### TRAIL SNACKS

Because of time constraints, or by preference, you may decide to snack during the day rather than stop for a meal break. The food you choose to take with you will be a matter of personal preference but it will also be dictated by the sort of climate you are travelling in. In hot countries, for instance, chocolate or anything with chocolate in it will melt and be very messy. Nuts, dried fruit, dried meat, biscuits and cheese are all suitable for eating on the move. Avoid salty foods that will simply make you thirsty. Some high-energy bars may not be to everybody's taste, so try them out before you set out on your expedition.

If you do decide to eat trail snacks make sure that any wrappings are not thrown away: put them into your pocket until you find a waste bin to throw them away.

◀ *Dried fruit and nuts are high-energy snacks and are easy to eat on the trail.*

▼ *Cereal bars are sustaining and can be substitutes for breakfast if necessary.*

▲ *Chocolate gives a quick burst of energy but it can make you thirsty.*

### PACK SIZE

Although it is a more expensive way to buy food, you may consider buying some things packed in individual portions, including coffee, sugar and creamer. These little packs will help with portion control and, as many are plastic, they will offer some protection against wet, damp, dust, sand and insects. The downside is that you have more packaging to get rid of.

The alternative is to pack up your own individual portions. Apart from specially sealed pouch meals, you can repackage cereals, pasta, soup and pudding mixes in light, small freezer bags, which you can recycle later to carry away litter. Don't forget to add labels to your packages identifying the ingredients and including any necessary cooking instructions.

### DRINKS

Tea, coffee and drinking chocolate are all light and easy to carry, and adding sugar to hot drinks will increase your calorie intake.

The most important drink is of course water. If you are living mainly on dehydrated food, it is important to make sure you are drinking enough fluid during the day, especially if it is hot and you are working hard. You can buy supplements from chemists which you can add to your water bottle, to put back into the body many of the trace elements which you will be losing if you are sweating a lot.

### ADDITIONS TO YOUR MENU

If you come across berries on bushes or other natural fruit, or carry some dried fruit with you, this can turn a rather bland dehydrated pudding into a great treat. If you pick wild fruit, you must always be confident that you have identified it correctly before you eat it, especially when travelling abroad, and be sure you know that it is edible and not poisonous. If you do find ripe berries to pick, try to avoid bushes growing beside busy roads as they tend to get coated with pollutants from the exhaust of passing vehicles. No matter where you get your wild food from, wash it before you eat it.

# Clean Water

When living outdoors, clean water will be the most important single item that will determine where you can go and for how long. You may have to plan your route and campsites to take into account the availability of water.

## FINDING WATER

The first thing to do is to look at the countryside around you for signs of streams, rivers, lakes or the sea. If you are in the desert, look for vegetation, which requires some water to survive. Also look in dried-up watercourses or at the base of cliffs, as water has previously flowed here, and even if you cannot see it you may find it by digging down 60–90cm/2–3ft.

If you are near the coast, by digging above the high water line you will soon

▼ *It is a good idea to equip yourself with more than one method of treating your drinking water.*

▲ *For your own safety you should always treat all water as potentially contaminated, even when travelling in wild areas.*

find a little pool of slightly salty but still drinkable water. Fresh water is lighter than salt water, so drink from the top of the pool. (Always remember that you should never be tempted to drink seawater itself under any circumstances, as its saltiness will quickly lead you to become dehydrated.) In rivers where

there is a lot of silt, the deeper down you get your water, the cleaner it will be, as most of the silt and debris travels in the top layer of fast-moving water. Remove any remaining silt and debris before purifying the water by pouring it through either a finely woven, sock-shaped filter bag or an ordinary sock filled with a layer of sand and then a layer of small pebbles.

▼ *A Millbank filter bag will remove some impurities from water, but not all.*

| CONTAMINATING ORGANISMS | | | |
|---|---|---|---|
| Methods of purification | Protozoans (5–15 microns) | Bacteria (0.2–10 microns) | Viruses (0.004–0.1 microns) |
| Boiling | Kills | Kills | Kills |
| Iodine | Does not kill all | Kills | Kills |
| Chlorine | Not effective on larger micro-organisms | Kills | Kills |
| Silver | Does not kill all | Kills | Does not kill all |
| Filters | Eliminates | Eliminates if pores are small enough | Does not eliminate |
| Purifier | Kills | Kills | Kills |

▲ *Boiling water kills all impurities and is the best way to make sure that it is safe for all purposes, including drinking.*

## PURIFYING WATER

The chart on the opposite page shows the benefits and disadvantages of all the methods of cleaning water. Once it has been purified, drinking water should always be kept in clean, sealed containers, labelled to avoid confusion.

## BOILING

The safest way to purify water is to boil it vigorously for at least 5 minutes and allow it to cool before drinking. If, however, you want water quickly or in large quantities, you might choose another method.

## CHEMICAL TREATMENTS

There are three different chemical agents currently used to treat water: iodine, chlorine and silver. When using any of these, always read the directions on the packet or bottle as in some cases an overdose can be harmful.

### Iodine

This is available in liquid form or as tablets. After treatment with iodine, the water should be left to stand for 20–30 minutes. Neutralizing tablets can take away most of the smell and taste.

Iodine should be used on a short-term basis only, and should be avoided by pregnant women, children or anyone with a thyroid condition.

### Chlorine

This is easy to use and takes only about 10 minutes to sterilize reasonably clean water and 30 minutes for more suspect water. Neutralizing tablets are available to take away most of the swimming-pool taste of chlorinated water.

### Silver

This may be less effective than the other chemicals, but is longer-lasting and leaves no taste. The sterilization process may take at least two hours.

▼ *A water purifier is simple and quick to use. Fill with water and leave to stand before pouring out drinking water.*

## FILTERS AND PURIFIERS

A purifier both filters and sterilizes the water, giving safe drinkable water, whereas a filter only sieves the water, which then needs to be chemically treated or boiled.

When choosing a filter, you need to know if it will filter enough water for the trip (you will need 2–3 litres/ 3½–5¼ pints per person per day in temperate climates, and up to 6 litres/ 10½ pints in extreme hot climates, more if you are working hard). You should also check to see how fast it works. For a purifier, you need to know how fast it works and whether the cartridge can be cleaned, or a new cartridge fitted. Disposable cartridges tend to be compact but involve more expense.

▼ *Water filters need thorough cleaning and servicing after use or they can become ineffective.*

# Striking Camp

When it comes to striking camp, it is important to have a proper system for dismantling everything so that everyone knows what they are doing. How complex the job is will depend on whether you are taking down a small overnight camp or a large base camp. The most important thing is to clear the campsite so as to leave no trace of your presence after you have gone.

### OVERNIGHT CAMPS

If the weather is fine, dismantle your tent first and hang it up to air while you are dealing with everything else. Pack all the rest of your gear into your backpack, then fold up your tent and add it to your pack.

If it is raining, pack your backpack first, while you are inside your tent, then pack the tent and add it to your pack. Make sure you dry the tent at the earliest opportunity (see below). When

▼ *In a large camp set up a system and have somewhere where you can stow equipment and baggage that has already been packed.*

▲ *Ideally, pack the tent away when it is dry and clean. If you have to put it away wet, unpack it and dry it as soon as you can.*

you have finished packing, spend a little time walking around the site to see if anything has been left lying around before you depart.

### BASE CAMPS

The size of this type of camp and the number of people concerned will make dismantling the camp a more complex operation. Make sure that everybody is involved and knows which jobs they

▲ *The tent poles should be counted and checked for any damage, then packed away in their own bag.*

have to do, and when. It is a good idea to keep one tent up until everything else is done, so that as you take the other tents down and pack up your cooking and other equipment, and any constructions such as clotheslines, you can put everything in this tent. If it rains, this will also stop all your kit getting wet. Alternatively, have a large groundsheet ready to spread over the kit that has been packed if the weather becomes stormy.

### STRIKING TENTS

As with pitching tents, the way in which you take the tent down will depend on the type of tent, but there are some general rules that should be followed for all of them. If you are taking down a large tent, make sure there are enough people working with you to take it down safely, so that the tent is not damaged.

When you strike your tent you may need to pack it up while it is wet. If you leave it for more than a few days, however, a cotton tent may become mildewed and a synthetic tent can start to smell (its cotton inner will also become mildewed), so get it dried as soon as possible.

If the tent has a sewn-in groundsheet, clean the inner tent thoroughly then turn the inner tent over to make sure the groundsheet is dry and clean. If not, let it dry then clean the groundsheet with a cloth.

▲ *Clean all your pegs so that they are ready for use next time. Make sure none has been left in the ground before you go.*

Make sure all the tent pegs are clean and straight and ready for use next time, and that you have the right number. Also check that all the guy lines and pegging points are in working order and any zips are working.

When you have taken down the tent, make sure that all the different parts, such as poles and pegs, are together in their respective bags before packing them away in the main bag.

### COOKING AREA
Make sure you fill in all the pits you have dug. If you have been using a fire, make sure it is out and that the fireplace has been filled in and the ground covering replaced.

### TOILETS
If you have set up your own toilets, make sure that all waste products are well buried, holes or trenches are filled in and the ground cover is replaced. All screening materials, unless they are naturally growing in the area, should be removed.

If you have dug a latrine and used it for some time, mark the site before you go so that others following you will not use the same site.

### WASTE
Either burn all the waste and bury the residue, or take it away with you. Never leave plastic bin liners full of waste at a site, as animals will quickly

rip them open, allowing the contents to blow away. If the animals try to eat the plastic, it can kill them.

Finally, it is a good idea to walk around the site once everything has been taken down and packed to see if any items of kit, any tent pegs or pieces of litter have been left lying about. There is nearly always something.

▲ *If the weather is dry and sunny, turn your groundsheet over to dry it off and clean it before packing up your tent. Pack your other equipment while it is airing.*

▼ *Make sure all your equipment is clean and dry before you pack it so that it is ready to use when you arrive at your next stopping place.*

# Index